I0459192

Quick Travel Guide to

Rome

By

Sarah M. Melland

Copyright © 2023
Published by Ripe Melland Media

All rights reserved. No part of this publication may be reproduced, stored in a retrieval system, or transmitted, in any form or by any means, electronic, mechanical, photocopying, recording, or otherwise, without the prior written permission of the publisher.

The Contents

Introduction

According to mythology, Rome was established in 753 B.C. by Romulus and Remus, the god of battle Mars' twin sons In 753 B.C., after being abandoned in a basket on the Tiber by a king of nearby Alba Longa and saved by a she-wolf, the twins lived to vanquish that monarch and create their own city on the river's banks. After murdering his brother, Romulus became the first ruler of Rome, which bears his name. A non-hereditary sequence of Sabine, Latin, and Etruscan (previous Italian civilizations) kings followed. Romulus, Numa Pompilius, Tullus Hostilius, Ancus Martius, Lucius Tarquinius Priscus (Tarquin the Elder), Servius Tullius, and Tarquinius Superbus, or Tarquin the Proud, are the seven mythological rulers of Rome (534-510 B.C.).

The monarchy of Rome ended in 509 B.C. After the deposition of its seventh monarch, Lucius Tarquinius Superbus, who was depicted by ancient historians as brutal and dictatorial in comparison to his beneficent predecessors. A popular rebellion was claimed to have erupted in response to the king's son's rape of a virtuous noblewoman, Lucretia. Whatever the reason, Rome evolved from a monarchy to a republic, a world based on res publica, or "people's property."

The "seven hills of Rome" are E'quili'e Hill, Palatine Hill, Aventine Hill, Capitoline Hill, Quirinal Hill, Viminal Hill and Caelian Hill.

Amazing History of Rome

The Roman Empire's history may be split into three separate periods: the Kings Period (625-510 BC), Republican Rome (510-31 BC), and Imperial Rome (31 BC – AD 476).

Founding (c. 625 BC)

Rome was built approximately 625 BC in the ancient Italian regions of Etruria and Latium. In reaction to an Etruscan invasion, it is assumed that Latium villagers joined forces with inhabitants from the surrounding hills to build the city-state of Rome. It is uncertain whether they banded together in defense or in response to being subjected to Etruscan control. Archaeological evidence suggests that a significant amount of transformation and unity occurred around 600 BC, leading to the founding of Rome as a genuine metropolis.

Period of Kings (625-510 BC)

The Period of Kings was the first period in Roman history, lasting from the establishment of Rome until 510 BC. During this brief period, Rome expanded militarily and economically, with growth in territorial limits, military prowess, and manufacture and sale of products like as oil lamps. Politically, the early building of the Roman constitution occurred during this time. The collapse of Etruscan dominance marked the end of the Period of Kings, ushering in Rome's Republican Period.

Republican Rome (510-31 BC)

In 510 BC, Rome began its Republican Period. The Romans constructed a new type of governance in which the top classes, particularly the senators and equestrians, or knights, governed. In times of crisis, though, a dictator may be nominated. The Romans constructed the "Twelve Tables" in 451 BC, an uniform system of rules for public, private, and political concerns.

During the Republican Period, Rome expanded farther, eventually gaining control of the whole Italian peninsula by 338 BC. The Punic Wars, which lasted from 264 to 146 BC, as well as some battles with Greece, enabled Rome to seize control of Carthage and Corinth and so become the main naval force in the Mediterranean.

Soon after, Rome's political climate pushed the Republic into anarchy and civil conflict. As a result, a dictator, L., was elected. Cornelius Sulla ruled from 82 to 80 BC. Following Sulla's departure in 79 BC, the Republic fell into disarray. While Rome remained a Republic for another 50 years, the transition to Imperialism began in 60 BC, when Julius Caesar ascended to power.

By 51 BC, Julius Caesar had conquered Celtic Gaul, and Rome's frontiers had expanded beyond the Mediterranean area for the first time. Although the Senate remained Rome's ruling body, its influence was dwindling. Julius Caesar was slain in 44 BC, and his heir, Gaius Julius Caesar Octavianus (Octavian), took his place. In 31 BC, Rome conquered Egypt, killing Mark Antony and establishing Octavian as Rome's unrivaled emperor. Octavian took the title Augustus and so became Rome's first emperor.

Imperial Rome (31 BC – AD 476)

The Imperial Period in Rome was its last, spanning from the ascension of Rome's first emperor in 31 BC through the destruction of Rome in AD 476. Rome saw several decades of peace,  wealth, and expansion throughout this time. By AD 117, the Roman

Empire had expanded to encompass three continents, including Asia Minor, northern Africa, and the majority of Europe.

The Roman Empire was divided into eastern and western empires in AD 286, each headed by its own emperor. The western empire was subjected to multiple Gothic invasions and was devastated by Vandals in AD 455.

After then, Rome continued to deteriorate until the Western Roman Empire collapsed in AD 476. The Byzantine Empire, often known as the Eastern Roman Empire, lasted until the 15th century AD. In AD 1453, Turks gained possession of its capital city, Constantinople (modern-day Istanbul in Turkey).

After the Fall (AD 476 – 800)

Following the collapse of the Western Roman Empire in AD 476, Rome came under the control of a succession of foreign powers. The city endured invasions from Germanic tribes such as the Ostrogoths and Lombards. Although its political influence waned, Rome remained a

vital spiritual center as Christianity grew in power. The popes gradually filled the leadership void left by the empire's collapse, guiding not only religion but also diplomacy and education.

The Holy Roman Empire and Papal Power (800–1300)

In AD 800, Pope Leo III crowned Charlemagne as Emperor of the Romans, marking the birth of the Holy Roman Empire. Though based north of the Alps, the empire sought to revive Rome's imperial legacy. Within the city itself, the papacy became both a religious and political force, constructing magnificent basilicas and defending territories known as the Papal States. During this era, Rome transformed into the beating heart of medieval Christendom, drawing pilgrims from across Europe.

Renaissance Rome (1300–1600)

After centuries of turbulence, Rome flourished once again during the Renaissance. Popes such as Julius II and Leo X commissioned artistic masterpieces that would define Western culture. Michelangelo painted the Sistine Chapel ceiling, Raphael decorated the Vatican's chambers, and Bramante designed St. Peter's Basilica. Rome became a dazzling showcase of human creativity and divine ambition. A city of learning,  architecture, and artistic rebirth. Yet beneath the beauty, political rivalries and foreign invasions continued, including the brutal Sack of Rome in 1527 by troops of Emperor Charles V.

Sarah Melland

From Papal States to Modern Italy (1600–1870)

The centuries that followed saw the papacy maintain control over central Italy, even as new European powers rose and fell. Baroque Rome emerged in the 1600s with grand fountains, palaces, and churches that still define the city's landscape. In the 19th century, revolutionary movements swept across Europe. The Kingdom of Italy was proclaimed in 1861, and in 1870, the Italian army entered Rome, ending papal rule. Rome was declared the capital of unified Italy, symbolizing a new era of national identity.

Twentieth Century and Beyond (1870–Present)

In 1929, the Lateran Treaty established the Vatican City as an independent sovereign state within Rome, resolving tensions between the papacy and the Italian government. During World War II, Rome endured Nazi occupation but was spared large-scale destruction. After the war, Italy transitioned into a republic in 1946, and Rome once again became a global capital, this time of art, diplomacy, and film. The 1950s and 1960s marked a new "La Dolce Vita" period, with Rome emerging as a symbol of postwar glamour and creativity.

Today, Rome stands as a living museum, a city where ancient ruins, Renaissance palaces, and modern life coexist. From emperors to popes, conquerors to artists, every era has left its mark on the Eternal City, ensuring that Rome's story never truly ends.

Fun Facts about Rome

Rome may be ancient, but it never stops surprising those who visit. Beneath its grand ruins and Renaissance splendor lies a city full of quirky stories, hidden laws, and centuries-old traditions that continue to shape daily life. From feline citizens and stolen fountain fortunes to coffee rules and ancient curiosities, here are some of the most fascinating and unusual facts about the Eternal City you probably didn't know.

#1 Rome is one of the most visited cities in the world

Rome is the most visited city in Italy and one of the most popular destinations for international visitors. Over 9.7 million people visited Rome in 2018.

#2 There's a country located inside Rome

Despite being only 4,700,000 square feet in size and officially the world's smallest nation, the Vatican City is its own autonomous country. It even has its own stamps and passports.

#3 The Pope doesn't live in Rome

If you were asked where the Pope lived, you would almost certainly respond Rome. In reality, his address is in Vatican City. The Pope is the leader of the country, which is ruled as an absolute monarchy.

#4 Someone took advantage of the Trevi Fountain's wealth

In 2002, Roberto Cecelletta was jailed for collecting coins from the famous fountain with a tiny fishing net, a rake, and a magnet. He'd been doing it for 34 years, earning approximately 850 Euros on certain days.

#6 Cats have their own laws in Rome

It is estimated that there are over 300,000 cats in Rome, and it turns out

that they have some pretty great rights as well. According to the 1991 biocultural heritage law, if five or more cats dwell together in a natural urban environment, they cannot be relocated. So now you know why there are so many kitty cats surrounding the Forum and the Colosseum!

#6 Rome didn't become a part of Italy until 1870

The unification of Italy occurred in the mid-nineteenth century, leading to the establishment of the Kingdom of Italy in 1861. Florence was the capital at the time. Rome was besieged by the Italian army in 1870 and became a part of the country (rather than being controlled by the Papacy). In 1871, the city was designated as the capital of the Kingdom of Italy.

#7 Even the ancient Romans loved to shop

We all know that Italians adore fashion, but you might be astonished to discover that the first shopping mall was established in Rome between 107 and 110 AD. Visit Trajan's Market to explore the ruins of the ornate arcade.

#8 Don't order a cappuccino after 11am in Rome

This is one of those stories told by friends and relatives to visitors to Rome. "Whatever you do, don't order a cappuccino after 11 a.m.; it's not cool!" "First and foremost, you may order one and Italians will not be astonished. However, the second reason is all about digestion. Because Italians believe that fresh milk is unhealthy for digestion, they prefer plain espressos later in the day or after a meal.

#9 Rome is home to one of the smallest inhabited islands in the world

The Tiber River runs through Rome, and inside it lies a little island known as Isola Tiberina (Tiber Island). It's just 270 metres long, therefore it's rather little. However, it is easily accessible through two bridges — the Ponte Cestio and Ponte Fabricio. Fatebenefratelli, a 16th-century hospital, is located on the island.

#10 The majority of Ancient Rome hasn't been excavated yet

While remarkable discoveries have been uncovered during excavations in Rome, around 90% of the old city is buried 30 feet below street level. Discoveries are still being discovered, but it's doubtful that much of the city will ever be unearthed because the present city's structures are built on top.

#11 There's a street that looks like London in the city of Rome

La Piccola Londra (Little London) was created by architect Quadrio Pirani in the early 1900s and is located in the Flaminio neighborhood. The 200-metre-long residential street is lined with colorful terraced buildings and steps going up to front doors. You may view it for yourself by going to Via Bernardo Celentano.

#12 All roads lead to Rome... sort of!

All roads lead to Rome is a well-known proverb, and it was once true! During the Roman Empire, all 80,000 km of roads stretched forth from the city, connecting many regions of the world, from Britain to Turkey. Many of these paths are still in use today.

A recent mapping research revisited the statement and plotted out 400,000 beginning places across Europe, discovering that all paths could still reach Rome today... thus I think the term is still relevant!

#13 Rome has a few delicacies that might turn your stomach

The culinary scene in Italy is popular with tourists, but there are a few local specialties that may not be to everyone's taste. Tripa alla Romana is a popular local dish that originated as peasant fare but has now become a staple of Roman cuisine. Tripe (cow gut lining) is carefully cooked in a delectable Italian tomato sauce and topped with pecorino cheese. It's tastier than it sounds, according to everyone!

#14 Ancient Rome had a few delicacies too

While the tripe may not be to your liking, wait till you hear what ancient people ate. The city's wealthiest dined on extravagant dinners of stork, ostrich, and even flamingo. Even a cute kittle dormouse was vulnerable, they preferred those loaded with meat!

#15 Even the medicine was gruesome in Ancient Rome

Gladiator blood was a popular treatment that doctors recommended for a variety of ailments. It was thought to possess extra-special qualities. Having difficulty conceiving? Consume some gladiator blood. Do you have epilepsy? Pour yourself a goblet of gladiator blood. Who knows if it was effective, but you won't find it at any pharmacy in Rome now!

#16 Rome is the city with the most churches

Rome has the most Christian cathedrals of any city in the world, with over 900 churches. Isn't it a fascinating truth about Rome?

#17 Rome is the city of fountains

One of the first things you will notice when seeing Rome is the abundance of fountains. Did you know any of these fascinating Rome facts?

Rome is also known as the "City of Fountains" since it contains over 2000 fountains. Many of them date from ancient periods through the Renaissance period, spanning roughly 2000 years.

They were created for much than simply decoration, and include the massive Trevi and Quattro Fiumi fountains. During the ancient Roman Empire, the first fountains were erected to transport water from outside the city via aqueducts.

With the collapse of the empire, they fell into disrepair and were resurrected in the 15th century to become decorative objects, with the building of spectacular carved marble fountains portraying Rome's rich culture and history.

#18 Home to the largest university in Europe

The city is home to the largest university in Europe that is also the second-largest in the world. La Sapienza University considered one of the most prestigious educational institutions, has many feathers in its cap.

Also called the University of Rome, the institution has given many famous scientists, politicians and Nobel prize laureates to the world.

#19 The best place for coffee lovers

One of the many facts about Italy is how famous it is for coffee. And what better place than the beautiful capital dotted with cute cafes to try out your favorite coffee?

Cappuccino is the favorite among the locals, and you will probably the best version of this in most parts of the city! But there are some coffee traditions like no Cappuccino is served after 11 AM or Espresso is the only coffee you can find if you want to have one after dinner.

#20 Rome is home to an ancient lie detector

The *Bocca della Verità*, or "Mouth of Truth," is an ancient marble mask carved in the likeness of a human face with hollow eyes, nose, and an open mouth. Dating back to the 1st century AD, it originally served as a drain cover or part of a fountain in the nearby Forum Boarium. Over time, it became one of Rome's most famous legends.

According to medieval folklore, the sculpture could detect lies. Anyone who told an untruth while placing their hand inside its mouth would have it bitten off. The myth transformed the simple stone disc into a symbol of honesty and divine justice. The sculpture now rests in the portico of the Church of Santa Maria in Cosmedin, where curious visitors still test their luck by slipping a hand inside and posing for photos. A ritual made world-famous by Audrey Hepburn and Gregory Peck in *Roman Holiday*.

Useful Italian Phrases

There are a few letters and sounds you might not be familiar with, so here's a quick pronunciation guide:

- **c** before *e* or *i* = "ch" (as in *ciao* or *certo*)
- **ch** before *e* or *i* = "k" (as in *chianti*)
- **g** before *e* or *i* = "j" (as in *gelato*)
- **gh** before *e* or *i* = hard "g" (as in *spaghetti*)
- **gli** = sounds like "lli" in *million* (softly blended)
- **gn** = "ny" (as in *lasagna*)
- **r** = lightly rolled or tapped with the tongue
- **sc** before *e* or *i* = "sh" (as in *scienza*)

Even though many Italians, especially in cities, speak some English, learning a few basic Italian phrases will help you connect more deeply and will always earn you a smile.

Greetings

- Good morning – **Buongiorno**
- Good afternoon / Good day – **Buon pomeriggio**
- Good evening – **Buonasera**
- Good night – **Buonanotte**
- Hello / Hi – **Ciao** (used among friends or informally any time of day)
- Goodbye – **Arrivederci** (formal) or **Ciao / A presto** (informal "see you soon")

Being Polite

- Thank you – **Grazie**
- You're welcome – **Prego**
- Please – **Per favore**
- Excuse me / Sorry – **Mi scusi** (formal) or **Scusa** (informal)

Introducing Yourself

- I am John – **Mi chiamo John** ("My name is John")
- I am from California – **Vengo dalla California**

- Nice to meet you – **Piacere di conoscerti**
- How are you? – **Come stai?** (informal) / **Come sta?** (formal)
- I'm fine, thank you – **Sto bene, grazie**

Common expressions using *sono* (I am):

- I am happy – **Sono felice**
- I am tired – **Sono stanco/stanca**
- I am hungry – **Ho fame**
- I am lost – **Mi sono perso/persa**

Asking for Things

- I want – **Vorrei** (polite) or **Voglio** (more direct)
- I want water – **Vorrei dell'acqua**
- I want to eat – **Vorrei mangiare**
- I want to go – **Vorrei andare**
- I want a souvenir – **Vorrei un souvenir**

Counting

- 1 – **uno**
- 2 – **due**
- 3 – **tre**
- 4 – **quattro**
- 5 – **cinque**
- 6 – **sei**
- 7 – **sette**
- 8 – **otto**
- 9 – **nove**
- 10 – **dieci**
- 100 – **cento**
- 1,000 – **mille**
- First – **Primo / Prima**
- Second – **Secondo / Seconda**
- Third – **Terzo / Terza**

Asking for Directions

- Right – **Destra**
- Left – **Sinistra**
- Straight ahead – **Dritto**
- Turn back – **Indietro**
- Where is – **Dov'è…?**
- Where is the cathedral? – **Dov'è la cattedrale?**
- Where is the hotel? – **Dov'è l'hotel?**
- Where is the train station? – **Dov'è la 23tazione?**
- Where is the bathroom? – **Dov'è il bagno?**

Café & Restaurant Phrases

Dining in Italy is a cultural experience. Meals are meant to be enjoyed slowly, often with wine and good company. Whether you're ordering a quick espresso or sitting down for a three-course dinner, these phrases will help you sound like a local and navigate menus with confidence.

At the Café

- A coffee, please – **Un caffè, per favore**
- A cappuccino, please – **Un cappuccino, per favore**
- An espresso – **Un espresso**
- With milk – **Con latte**
- Without sugar – **Senza Zucchero**
- A glass of water – **Un bicchiere d'acqua**
- To go / Takeaway – **Da portare via**

At the Restaurant

- A table for two, please – **Un tavolo per due, per favore**
- Do you have a reservation? – **Avete una prenotazione?**
- Yes, I have a reservation – **Sì, ho una prenotazione**
- The menu, please – **Il 24taz, per favore**
- The wine list, please – **La carta dei vini, per favore**
- What do you recommend? – **Cosa mi consiglia?**
- I'll have this one – **Prendo questo**
- I'm vegetarian – **Sono 24tazione24n / vegetariana**
- No meat, please – **Senza carne, per favore**
- No fish, please – **Senza pesce, per favore**
- I'm allergic to… – **Sono allergico / allergica a…**

Ordering & Eating

- I would like… – **Vorrei…**
- The same, please – **Lo stesso, per favore**
- This is delicious! – **È delizioso!**
- Cheers! – **Salute!**
- Enjoy your meal – **Buon 24tazione!**

Paying the Bill

- The bill, please – **Il conto, per favore**
- Can we pay separately? – **Possiamo pagare separatamente?**
- Do you take credit cards? – **Accettate carte di credito?**
- Keep the change – **Tenga il resto**
- Thank you for the meal – **Grazie per il pranzo / la cena**

Quick Tips

- In Italy, coffee is typically enjoyed **standing at the bar**, and it's cheaper than sitting at a table.
- Tipping isn't required; service is often included in the bill (*servizio incluso*). Rounding up or leaving small change is appreciated.
- Dinner starts late, most locals dine after 8 p.m.

Shopping & Money Phrases

From open-air markets to luxury boutiques, shopping in Italy is both an art and a pleasure. Knowing a few key phrases will help you browse, ask prices, and make purchases with confidence.

General Shopping

- How much does it cost? – **Quanto costa?**
- It's too expensive – **È troppo caro / cara**
- Do you have something cheaper? – **Avete qualcosa di più economico?**
- I'm just looking – **Sto solo guardando**
- I'll take it – **Lo prendo / La prendo**
- Do you have this in another size? – **Avete questo in un'altra 25tazio?**
- Do you have this in another color? – **Avete questo in un altro colore?**
- Can I try it on? – **Posso provarlo / provarla?**
- Where are the fitting rooms? – **Dove 25tazio camerini?**

At the Market

- How much are these tomatoes? – **Quanto costano questi pomodori?**
- I'd like a kilo of oranges – **Vorrei un chilo di arance**
- Can you make it a little less? – **Può farmi uno sconto?**
- Fresh – **Fresco / Fresca**
- Delicious – **Delizioso / Deliziosa**

- That's enough, thank you – **Basta così, grazie**

Paying & Money

- Do you take credit cards? – **Accettate carte di credito?**
- Can I pay in cash? – **Posso pagare in contanti?**
- Where is the ATM? – **Dov'è il bancomat?**
- I need to change money – **Devo cambiare dei soldi**
- How much is this souvenir? – **Quanto costa questo souvenir?**
- Receipt, please – **Lo scontrino, per favore**

Useful Words

- Sale – **Saldi**
- Discount – **Sconto**
- Shop – **Negozio**
- Open – **Aperto**
- Closed – **Chiuso**
- Price – **Prezzo**
- Cash register – **Cassa**
- Credit card – **Carta di credito**

Quick Tips

- Most shops close for a few hours in the afternoon (*pausa pranzo*) between 1:00 p.m. and 4:00 p.m.
- During the official **saldi** seasons (January–February and July–August), prices can drop dramatically.
- Always ask for a receipt (*scontrino*) when shopping; it's required by Italian law.

Transportation & Getting Around

Rome's streets can feel like a beautiful maze, ancient ruins next to modern roundabouts, but getting around is easier once you know a few essential phrases. Whether you're taking the metro, catching a bus, or asking for a taxi, these expressions will help you move through the city with ease.

Public Transportation

- Where is the metro station? – **Dov'è la 27tazione della metropolitana?**

- Where is the bus stop? – **Dov'è la fermata dell'autobus?**

- Which line goes to the Colosseum? – **Quale 27tazione al Colosseo?**

- Where can I buy a ticket? – **Dove posso comprare un biglietto?**

- I need a ticket – **Ho bisogno di un biglietto**

- One ticket, please – **Un biglietto, per favore**

- Return ticket – **Biglietto di andata e ritorno**

- How much is a ticket? – **Quanto costa un biglietto?**

- Does this bus go to Termini Station? – **Questo autobus va alla 27tazione Termini?**

By Taxi or Car

- I need a taxi – **Ho bisogno di un taxi**

- Can you call a taxi, please? – **Può chiamare un taxi, per favore?**

- How much to go to the airport? – **Quanto costa per andare all'aeroporto?**

- To the city center, please – **Al centro, per favore**

- Stop here, please – **Si fermi qui, per favore**

- Can you wait for me? – **Può aspettarmi?**

- Keep the change – **Tenga il resto**

By Train

- Where is the train station? – **Dov'è la 27tazione ferroviaria?**

- I would like a ticket to Florence – **Vorrei un biglietto per Firenze**

- What time does the train leave? – **A che ora parte il treno?**
- Which platform? – **Qual binario?**
- Is this the train to Naples? – **È il treno per Napoli?**

By Foot or Scooter

- Is it far from here? – **È lontano da qui?**
- Can I walk there? – **Posso andare a piedi?**
- I'm lost – **Mi sono perso / persa**
- I need a map – **Mi serve una mappa**
- I want to rent a scooter – **Voglio noleggiare uno scooter**
- How much does it cost per hour? – **Quanto costa all'ora?**

Useful Words

- Ticket – **Biglietto**
- Station – **Stazione**
- Bus – **Autobus**
- Train – **Treno**
- Metro – **Metropolitana**
- Taxi – **Taxi**
- Airport – **Aeroporto**
- Stop – **Fermata**
- Platform – **Binario**

Quick Tips

- Always validate your ticket before boarding buses, trams, or trains using the yellow or green machines.
- Rome's metro has only three main lines (A, B, and C), but they connect all major attractions.

For airport transfers, official taxis have a fixed fare to central Rome. Avoid unmarked cars.

Italian Etiquette Tips

Italians take pride in style, manners, and tradition. Qualities that extend to every meal and social interaction. Understanding a few basic customs will help you blend in gracefully, whether you're enjoying a coffee at a local bar or dining at a fine restaurant. Small gestures of respect, punctuality, and politeness go a long way in Italy's culture of *la bella figura*, "making a good impression."

Dress

- Italians prefer to create a good first impression ("la bella figura"), so dress appropriately. In English, see the British Debrett's guide on appropriate clothes for certain events (there will be slight differences but nothing exceptional).

- Men must wear a suit jacket, decent trousers, a button up collared shirt, closed shoes, and occasionally a tie to formal meals. Jeans or casual pants and a shirt are appropriate for casual eateries. For a formal supper, ladies should wear a good dress or outfit (no glittery, flashy, or black lace apparel throughout the day) and a great relaxed attire for less formal places. Tracksuits, other sportswear, and pajamas are often not worn out to dine.

Entering

- Arrive on time.
- Ladies may enter first, and the entrance is held open for them. They are helped to remove their jackets and carry their luggage.
- During the day (and later as one travels south in Italy), the traditional greeting is "Buon giorno." Allow the restaurant personnel to welcome you first and return with the same greeting (buon giorno / buona sera) in the afternoon and evening.
- When greeting friends, Italians frequently "kiss" them on the cheeks while shaking hands. It is not a kiss, but rather pressing your cheek on the other person's left cheek and then repeating on the opposite side. Males typically do not kiss other men and instead shake hands. Close friends and relatives will embrace rather than shake hands as they "kiss" hello. Begin by placing your left cheek on their left cheek.
- When shaking hands in business, Italians never cross their hands since it is considered bad luck. (For example, if you and your colleague are standing next to each other and shake hands first with the person immediately opposite you and then with the person diagonal to you- you and your colleague let one go first before shaking hands with the next one.)
- In the evening, visitors are served an aperitivo, which is usually accompanied by small nibbles.

Service

- In Europe, excellent service is regarded an art form, and many individuals make a living as servers. Many servers take considerable pleasure in their work and are well-liked. In many casual restaurants in Italy, the waitresses are members of the same family that owns the establishment. Servers must be handled with dignity at all times. It's never a good idea to be nasty to the proprietor's daughter.

- Ladies are served first.
- Generally speaking, if you are kind and ask nicely, the servers will help you to order.
- Do not shout at the waiter, rise up, wave frantically, or get up and walk up to him. Simply raising your hand should enough as an indicator.
- Dishes are served from the left, while soiled dishes are picked up from the right.

Ordering

- When ready to order, close the menu as an indication to the waiter.
- Generally, everyone orders their own meal.
- Ladies are allowed to order first.

Top Attractions

From ancient ruins to Renaissance masterpieces, every corner of Rome tells a story. The city is a living museum layered with over two thousand years of history, where emperors, popes, and artists all left their mark. Whether you're wandering through centuries-old piazzas, gazing up at monumental domes, or savoring a gelato beneath a baroque fountain, these are the must-see highlights that capture the spirit of the Eternal City.

#1 The Colosseum

It is the largest amphitheater in the Roman world, seating more than 50,000 people. In these arenas, where the famed gladiatorial combats, animal fights, and Roman games were staged, much blood was spilt, invariably followed by tragic deaths.

The visit is not free, and you will most likely have to wait for several hours if you go during peak season.

#2 The Roman Forum

The ticket purchased at the Colosseum also covers entrance to the Roman Forum and the Palatine Hill (discussed further below), so it would be a pity to miss them, as the three tourist attractions are connected together.

The forum was the city's center, and there are relics of old marketplaces, governmental buildings, and religious structures. However, there is no explanation on the site, so if you're interested in history, you should take a guided tour.

I recommend the small group trip of the Colosseum, Roman Forum, and Palatine Hill. It is the most comprehensive and is accessible in English, Italian, Spanish, and French, which is really convenient!

#3 The Palatine Hill

This is the third attraction included with the Colosseum ticket.

Palatine Hill, one of Rome's seven hills, is said to be the site where Romulus and Remus established the city. They are, as you may remember, the two twins who would have been found and suckled by a wolf in a cave.

This cave and the remnants of historical persons' houses, such as Augustus, the first Roman emperor, are accessible from the summit of Palatine Hill.

#4 The Pantheon

The Pantheon is Rome's best surviving ancient edifice and yet another must-see tourist site!

It was originally dedicated to all mythological divinities before becoming a Christian church in the seventh century. Don't be afraid to enter; the visit is free, which is unusual enough to remark!

Inside, appreciate the massive dome and the oculus (the aperture in the dome that provides unique illumination).

There are also the graves of Raphael (the famed artist) and Victor Emmanuel II in the Pantheon (1st king of Italy, as mentioned above when I talked about the beautiful building dedicated to him on Piazza Venezia)

#5 Trevi Fountain

The most renowned fountain in Europe, the Trevi Fountain, is very near to the Pantheon (Fontana di Trevi in Italian). A must-see attraction for anybody visiting Rome.

This fountain is also known for holding a great amount of wedding proposals due to the mystique around it! According to legend, a young girl had to give the location of the spring to the Romans in order to save her virginity.

Numerous sculptures in the basin depict an allegory of the sea, with Neptune in his chariot in the center. According to custom, you should toss two coins: one to make a wish and the other to ensure your return to Rome.

A huge baroque mansion behind the fountain adds to the attractiveness of the site. Just one thing: the site is constantly busy, so taking a nice shot of the fountain with no unwanted heads will be difficult!

Nonetheless, the Trevi Fountain is a popular tourist attraction in Rome.

#6 Enjoy Gelato (Italian ice cream)

The fantastic news is that you're at an outstanding location, extremely close to one of Rome's two top ice cream stores, San Crispino on Via della Panatteria. The line is frequently stunning, but the finest things in life are the most difficult to achieve!

#7 Villa Borghese gardens

The largest and most beautiful public park in Rome is located north of Piazza di Spagna. After the congested streets and tourist attractions, the Villa Borghese gardens provide a nice respite! You'll be able to wander through broad, shaded lanes and along the  side of a lake surrounded by temples, sculptures, and several fountains. There is also a lovely botanical garden in the park. To access there, go to either the Porta Pinciana or the Piazzale Flaminio park gates.

#8 Rome's Famous Squares (Piazze di Roma)

Rome's piazzas are more than open spaces, they are the city's living rooms, where history, art, and everyday life intersect. From grand ceremonial centers to neighborhood gathering spots, each square tells its own story through architecture, fountains, and the rhythm of daily Roman life. Strolling from one to another is the best way to experience the city's vibrant heart.

Piazza Venezia

Piazza Venezia, one of Rome's great squares, is located not far from the Roman Forum, at the other end of Via dei Fori Impierali. All the streets lead to Rome's main tourist sites from there!

This is where you may see the Victor Emmanuel II Monument, also known as the "Altare della Patria" or "Vittoriano," a massive white marble structure dedicated to Italy's first king, Victor Emmanuel II.

Next to the square lies the famed Trajan's column, which features bas-reliefs depicting the Emperor Trajan's military triumphs.

The building's roof also provides an excellent panoramic view of the entire city. A glass elevator at the rear of the building provides access.

Piazza Navona

The Piazza Navona is located in the historic center, close to the Pantheon. It's one of Rome's most gorgeous and well-known squares! There, you may view the three fountains listed below:

- The Quattro Fiumi Fontana
- The Nettuno Fountain
- The Moro's Fontana

It's a nice area to take a drink or eat ice cream on one of the numerous terraces, but be aware that the costs are high because it's a popular tourist destination.

Piazza di Spagna

The Via Condotti will lead you directly to the picturesque Piazza di Spagna, which is undoubtedly one of the most popular squares due to the stunning view it provides.

The Piazza di Spagna lies at the base of the great stairway that leads to the Trinità dei Monti basilica. Tourists and Italians alike will enjoy a quick respite on the lovely staircase. A popular meeting spot!

On the Piazza, there is also the Barcaccia fountain, which contributes to the ambiance.

You could have a bite to eat and a beverage from the cafe and then lounge about the park's many corners. Aside from this, you may rent a bicycle from the park and have a leisurely spin around the grounds.

Piazza del Popolo

Once the northern gateway to the Eternal City, Piazza del Popolo, the "People's Square," is one of Rome's grandest open spaces. Designed in neoclassical style in the early 1800s, it is framed by twin Baroque churches and centered around an ancient

Egyptian obelisk that once stood in the Circus Maximus. Elegant fountains and sweeping symmetry give the square a sense of calm despite its size. From here, a short climb up the Pincio Terrace rewards visitors with one of the most spectacular panoramic views of Rome, especially at sunset when the city glows gold beneath the skyline of domes.

Campo de' Fiori

Vibrant and full of character, Campo de' Fiori transforms throughout the day. A bustling produce and flower market in the morning, and a lively hub of restaurants and bars at night. At its center stands the statue of philosopher

Giordano Bruno, executed here in 1600 for his revolutionary ideas. The mix of history, energy, and local color makes this one of Rome's most authentic squares.

Piazza della Repubblica

Located near Termini Station, Piazza della Repubblica is a sweeping circular square anchored by the *Fountain of the Naiads*, whose elegant bronze figures symbolize water nymphs. Behind the curved Renaissance arcades stands the *Basilica of St. Mary of the Angels and Martyrs*, designed by Michelangelo within the ruins of Diocletian's Baths, a striking fusion of ancient and modern.

Piazza della Rotonda

One of Rome's most atmospheric squares, Piazza della Rotonda sits before the Pantheon, the city's best-preserved ancient monument. Its central fountain, crowned by a slender Egyptian obelisk, sparkles against the temple's massive portico and granite columns. By day it's filled with sightseers and café tables; by night, it glows under lamplight, offering one of the most magical views in all of Rome.

Piazza del Campidoglio

Set atop the Capitoline Hill, Piazza del Campidoglio is one of Rome's most elegant and meaningful squares designed by Michelangelo in the 16th century as a masterpiece of urban harmony. Once the political and religious heart of ancient Rome, the site was reimagined during the Renaissance to face the new city rather than the ruins of the past. The piazza's graceful symmetry, geometric pavement pattern, and surrounding palaces create a sense of balance and grandeur that still feels timeless. At its center stands a replica of the ancient equestrian statue of Emperor Marcus Aurelius, with the original preserved in the nearby Capitoline Museums, among the oldest public museums in the world. From the rear terrace, visitors can enjoy one of Rome's most breathtaking views over the Roman Forum.

Piazza della Bocca della Verità

Located between the Forum Boarium and the Tiber River, Piazza della Bocca della Verità is one of Rome's most historically layered squares.

Its name comes from the famous *Bocca della Verità* ("Mouth of Truth"), an ancient marble mask housed in the portico of the nearby Church of Santa Maria in Cosmedin. According to legend, it bites the hand of anyone who tells a lie.

The square itself sits on what was once the city's ancient cattle market and is surrounded by some of Rome's oldest temples, including the Temple of Hercules Victor, a perfectly preserved circular marble temple and the Temple of Portunus, dedicated to the god of harbors. With its blend of myth, religion, and early Roman architecture, Piazza della Bocca della Verità feels like a small open-air museum and a quiet counterpart to the bustling Forum just beyond.

Pro Tips for Exploring Rome's Piazzas

Best time to visit: Early morning offers soft light and quiet streets, ideal for photos. Evenings bring out the city's magic, when musicians play, fountains sparkle, and cafés fill with locals.

Sunset views: For the best golden-hour panoramas, head to Pincio Terrace above Piazza del Popolo or the Trinità dei Monti viewpoint atop the Spanish Steps.

Café breaks: Enjoy espresso or gelato in Piazza Navona at Café Domiziano or Giolitti near the Pantheon. In Campo de' Fiori, grab an aperitivo at Obicà Mozzarella Bar and people-watch as the market transforms into nightlife.

Hidden corners: Piazza della Rotonda glows beautifully after dark, while Piazza della Repubblica offers elegant calm away from the crowds. For a quieter local vibe, try the charming lanes behind Piazza di Spagna or Piazza Venezia.

Getting around: Most squares are walkable from one another. Wear comfortable shoes, bring water, and follow the rhythm of the city. Rome is best explored slowly.

#9 The Four Papal Basilicas

No visit to Rome is complete without stepping inside its four Papal Basilicas. The most sacred and historically significant churches in the Catholic world. Each one holds a unique place in Rome's story, from the ancient foundations of Christianity to the heights of Renaissance art and Baroque architecture. Together, they form a spiritual pilgrimage across the city: from St. Peter's grandeur in the Vatican to the ancient majesty of St. John Lateran, the solemn beauty of St. Paul Outside the Walls, and the golden splendor of St. Mary Major. These basilicas are more than religious sites, they are living monuments to faith, history, and artistic genius.

St. Peter's Basilica (Basilica di San Pietro in Vaticano)

Featured in #15 Vatican City

St. John Lateran (Basilica di San Giovanni in Laterano)

The oldest and highest-ranking of all churches in Rome, St. John Lateran is the official cathedral of the city and the Pope's own church as Bishop of Rome. Founded by Emperor Constantine in the 4th century, it is often called the "Mother of All Churches." Its monumental façade and 12 colossal statues of the apostles give way to a richly decorated interior filled with mosaics and relics. Across the street stands the *Scala Sancta* (Holy Stairs), believed to be the steps Christ climbed during his trial before Pontius Pilate.

St. Paul Outside the Walls (Basilica di San Paolo Fuori le Mura)

Located along the ancient Via Ostiense, this vast basilica marks the burial place of St. Paul the Apostle. Founded by Emperor Constantine and rebuilt after a fire in the 19th century, it retains its solemn grandeur with a forest of columns, intricate mosaics and a serene cloister. Along the upper walls, portraits of every pope in history line the nave. A visual timeline of the Church's continuity. Despite its scale, it remains one of the most peaceful and contemplative sites in Rome.

St. Mary Major (Basilica di Santa Maria Maggiore)

The largest Marian church in Rome, Saint Mary Major blends early Christian architecture with Renaissance and Baroque splendor. Built in the 5th century after a miraculous snowfall supposedly revealed its location, the basilica dazzles with golden mosaics depicting biblical scenes and a ceiling gilded with the first gold from the New World. Beneath the altar rests a reliquary said to contain fragments of the Holy Crib, making this basilica a cherished site of devotion.

Some other interesting churches to see in Rome:

- Chiesa del Gesù
- Basilica di Santa Maria in Trastevere
- Basilica di San Clemente al Laterano
- Chiesa di Santa Maria della Concezione
- Chiesa di Sant'Ignazio di Loyola

#10 Go shopping in Rome

If you want to go shopping in Rome, now is the time: you're near to the two big shopping streets. Visit Via del Corso for some retail therapy.

If you have a higher budget or just want to admire the shop windows, continue your way on Via Condotti. It's the most prestigious street of Rome with brands like Gucci, Armani or Prada. A bit like the Champs Elysée in Paris!

#11 The Bridge and Castel Sant'Angelo

Following the Tiber from the plaza, you may reach the Sant'Angelo bridge and the fortress of the same name on the opposite bank.

Bernini sculpted the ten angel figurines that adorn the bridge. The view of the city and the river from the bridge is spectacular.

Emperor Hadrian, on the other hand, created the Castel Sant'Angelo to function as a tomb. Later on, it began to play a significant military function, even serving as a shelter for popes during invasions! They've even established direct contact to the Vatican.

You may tour the castle, as well as the graves and former popes' chambers. The amazing view from the rampart should not be overlooked.

#12 Trastevere District

This neighborhood is getting increasingly popular and "Hipster," yet for the time being it has preserved all of its unique charm.

You'll be (relatively) alone to explore its distinctive tiny and floral streets. There are no large historical monuments here, as there are in the rest of Rome, but rather a genuine "Italian" neighborhood with its population and local stores. Climb the Gianicolo hill on your route to the north of the area to see the view.

#13 San Lorenzo District

The San Lorenzo quarter is less well-known among tourists but is well worth a visit. Originally a working-class neighborhood, it is today a student neighborhood with Roman universities. It's a favored hangout for street artists as well as students. And the nightlife is fantastic for beginners, and beer is quite reasonably priced!

#14 Aventine Hill & the Keyhole View

The Aventine Hill ("Aventino" in Italian) offers a tranquil neighborhood, magnificent gardens, and an unrivaled perspective of the city to offer! It will also provide you with one of the most stunning views of Rome.

Piazza dei Cavalieri di Malta is home to the famed Aventine Keyhole. People will be waiting in line to peep through the keyhole.

#15 Vatican City

From the Castel Sant'Angelo to the Vatican is a lengthy hallway. Even if you are not religious, a visit to the Vatican is a must during your time in Rome.

It is the world's smallest nation, but it is one of the most popular stops on an Italian trip. Only priests and nuns, nobles, guards, and, of course, the Pope are permitted to reside there.

A little note regarding the guards: they are solely Swiss and must be Catholic. They take an oath of loyalty to the Pope.

The Swiss guards defended the pope on his retreat to the Sant'Angelo fortress during the fall of Rome in 1527.

What to See in Vatican City

Though Vatican City is the world's smallest sovereign state, it holds some of humanity's greatest achievements in art, architecture, and faith. Beyond the famous basilica, there's a wealth of treasures tucked behind its ancient walls.

1. St. Peter's Basilica

The largest church in the world and the spiritual heart of Catholicism. Its vast interior contains Michelangelo's *Pietà*, Bernini's bronze Baldacchino canopy, and the tombs of several popes. Climb to the top of the dome for a panoramic view of St. Peter's Square and the rooftops of Rome.

2. St. Peter's Square (Piazza San Pietro)

Designed by Gian Lorenzo Bernini, this grand oval piazza is embraced by sweeping colonnades meant to symbolize the open arms of the Church. The Egyptian obelisk at its center dates back 2,000 years and was moved here under Pope Sixtus V in 1586.

3. The Vatican Museums

A labyrinth of over 1,400 rooms filled with art, antiquities and masterpieces collected by the popes over centuries. Highlights include:

- **The Raphael Rooms** – A suite of four frescoed chambers painted by Raphael and his pupils.
- **The Gallery of Maps** – A long, gilded corridor lined with detailed 16th-century maps of Italy.
- **The Pio-Clementino Museum** – Showcases classical sculptures such as *Laocoön and His Sons* and *Apollo Belvedere*.
- **The Gregorian Egyptian and Etruscan Museums** – Dedicated to artifacts from ancient civilizations that shaped Rome.

4. The Sistine Chapel

The Sistine Chapel is the spiritual and artistic heart of the Vatican — the one place every visitor comes to see at least once in their lifetime. Completed in 1481 under Pope Sixtus IV (from whom it takes its name), the chapel was originally intended for papal ceremonies. Its walls were first decorated by Renaissance masters like Botticelli, Ghirlandaio, and Perugino, but it was Michelangelo's later work that transformed it into one of the greatest masterpieces in human history.

The ceiling, painted between 1508 and 1512, depicts scenes from the *Book of Genesis*, including the world-famous *Creation of Adam*, where God's outstretched finger gives life to man. More than 20 years later, Michelangelo returned to paint *The Last Judgment* behind the altar, a

monumental fresco of swirling figures and divine drama that still stuns viewers with its scale and intensity.

Beyond its beauty, the chapel remains deeply sacred. It is here that the College of Cardinals gathers in secrecy to elect each new pope, a process known as the *conclave*. The chapel's silence, illuminated only by the glow of frescoed color, offers an unforgettable reminder that art and faith are forever intertwined in the story of Rome.

5. The Vatican Gardens

Covering nearly half of the Vatican's territory, these private gardens are filled with fountains, grottoes, and centuries-old trees. Access is limited to guided tours, making it a peaceful retreat from the crowds.

6. The Vatican Necropolis (Scavi)

Beneath St. Peter's Basilica lies an ancient Roman burial ground believed to contain the tomb of St. Peter himself. Visits are by special reservation only through the Vatican Excavations Office. A rare and unforgettable experience.

7. The Apostolic Palace

The official residence of the Pope, the Apostolic Palace includes the Papal Apartments, the Vatican Library, and the Borgia Apartments decorated with Renaissance frescoes

by Pinturicchio. Though not fully open to the public, portions can be seen on certain museum routes.

8. The Vatican Library

One of the oldest libraries in the world, founded in 1475, holding over a million printed books and priceless manuscripts, including early maps, papal documents, and illuminated texts. Scholars can access it by appointment only, but its existence underscores the Vatican's role in preserving global knowledge.

9. The Vatican Post Office

With its own stamps and postal system, the Vatican Post is famous for its speed and reliability. Many visitors mail postcards from here to receive the distinctive Vatican postmark.

10. St. Peter's Dome Viewpoint

The climb to the dome (551 steps or elevator + stairs) offers one of the most spectacular views in Europe, looking down over the basilica's nave and out across the entire city of Rome.

Pro Tip:

Vatican City is busiest mid-morning. Arrive at the Vatican Museums before opening (around 8 a.m.) or book a skip-the-line ticket in advance. Dress modestly. Shoulders and knees should be covered inside all sacred sites.

#16 The Baths of Caracalla

The Baths of Caracalla (*Terme di Caracalla*) are among the largest and most remarkable ancient ruins in Rome, built between AD 212 and 216 under Emperor Caracalla. Once able to host over 1,600 bathers at a time, the complex functioned as both a public bathhouse and a social hub,

complete with gyms, gardens, and libraries. Though now in ruins, its towering arches, intricate floor mosaics, and massive brick halls still convey the scale and sophistication of Roman engineering. During the summer months, the site transforms into an open-air venue for concerts and operas, allowing visitors to experience history under the stars.

#17 The Catacombs of Rome

An underground network of early Christian burial tunnels stretching for miles beneath the city, haunting and fascinating to explore.

#18 The Appian Way (Via Appia Antica)

One of Rome's oldest roads, perfect for a scenic bike ride lined with ancient tombs, aqueducts and cypress trees.

#19 The Spanish Steps (Scalinata di Trinità dei Monti)

One of Rome's most photographed landmarks, the Spanish Steps link the elegant Piazza di Spagna below with the Trinità dei Monti church above. Built in the

18th century, the grand 135-step staircase was designed as a meeting point between French and Spanish communities in the city and quickly became a social hub. Today, it remains a favorite spot to pause with a gelato and admire the view of Via dei Condotti's fashion boutiques below, though sitting on the steps is now discouraged to preserve their beauty.

#20 Janiculum Hill (Gianicolo Hill)

Often called the "balcony of Rome," Janiculum Hill rises just beyond the Trastevere district and offers one of the most breathtaking panoramic views of the city. Though not one of Rome's original seven hills, it has long held strategic and symbolic importance. It was here that Garibaldi and his troops defended the newborn Italian Republic in 1849. Today, leafy promenades, statues of heroes, and the equestrian Monument to Garibaldi line its terraces. At noon each day, a cannon is

fired from the hill, a tradition dating back to the 19th century to help Romans keep time. Whether you come for the history, the shade of the pine trees, or the sweeping skyline views stretching from St. Peter's to the Colosseum, Janiculum Hill is one of the most peaceful and inspiring spots in Rome. Stop by the beautiful Fontana dell'Acqua Paola fountain while you are there.

Hidden Gems

Beyond the ruins, piazzas, and grand monuments that define Rome, there's another side to the Eternal City, quieter, quirkier, and every bit as captivating. Tucked between ancient walls and winding alleyways are forgotten tombs, secret viewpoints, artistic treasures, and cafés that locals keep to themselves. These hidden gems reveal Rome's soul: intimate, surprising, and layered with centuries of stories waiting to be discovered.

#1 Europe's Only Ancient Pyramid

Tucked beside the old Aurelian Walls stands a surprising sight. A perfectly preserved Egyptian-style pyramid, built more than 2,000 years ago as the tomb of Gaius Cestius, a wealthy Roman magistrate. The Pyramid of Cestius, about one-third the size of those in Giza, reflects the wave of "Egyptomania" that swept Rome after the conquest of Egypt. For centuries, locals believed it was the resting place of Remus, Rome's legendary founder, until archaeologists uncovered inscriptions revealing its true origin. Today it remains Europe's only ancient pyramid — an extraordinary fusion of Roman power and Egyptian fascination.

#2 The Protestant Cemetery (Cimetero Acattolico)

Next to the pyramid lies one of Rome's most peaceful sanctuaries, the Non-Catholic Cemetery. Shaded by cypress and pine trees, this serene garden is the final resting place of poets John Keats and Percy Bysshe Shelley, along with diplomats, artists, and scholars from across Europe. Marble sculptures, moss-covered tombs, and birdsong give the place a haunting beauty. As Shelley once wrote of it, "It might make one in love with death, to be buried in so sweet a place."

#3 Church of Sant Andrea della Valle

Among the hundreds of churches in Rome, Sant'Andrea della Valle often goes unnoticed. Its modest exterior conceals a breathtaking Baroque interior, where golden columns frame vast frescoes that rise toward one of the city's most magnificent domes. The church is also famed for its connection to opera, Puccini's *Tosca* begins here, and for its intricate ceiling paintings that rival those of the more crowded basilicas nearby.

#4 The Rooftop Bar at Martis Palace Hotel

Just steps from Piazza Navona, the rooftop terrace of the Martis Palace Hotel offers a 360-degree view of Rome's skyline without the crowds or inflated prices. As the sun sets, guests can enjoy a quiet drink while watching the domes and rooftops of the Eternal City turn gold. It's one of the few remaining panoramic spots in central Rome where locals and travelers alike can take in the view in peace.

#5 Palace of Justice (Palazzo di Giustizia)

Located along the Tiber River near the Vatican, the Palace of Justice is one of Rome's grandest late-19th-century buildings. Constructed between 1889 and 1911, it houses Italy's Supreme Court and the Judicial Public Library. Designed by architect Guglielmo Calderini, the massive structure is built from travertine stone and richly decorated with sculptures, Corinthian columns, and ornate friezes symbolizing law and order.

Nicknamed "Il Palazzaccio" ("The Ugly Palace") by locals for its imposing scale, it remains an architectural masterpiece of the post-unification era. The rooftop terrace offers sweeping views over the Tiber, Castel Sant'Angelo, and St. Peter's Basilica, making it one of Rome's most photogenic civic buildings, even if few visitors ever step inside.

#6 Eataly

Far from a typical supermarket, Eataly Roma is a cathedral of Italian cuisine spread across four floors near the Ostiense train station. Inside, you'll find artisan pastas, local wines, fresh cheeses, pastries, and small restaurants serving everything from handmade ravioli to espresso and cannoli. It's where food and culture meet. A one-stop showcase of Italy's culinary artistry.

#7 The Aventine Keyhole

On Aventine Hill, a small keyhole in the green doors of the Knights of Malta Priory reveals one of Rome's most astonishing perspectives: the dome of St. Peter's Basilica perfectly framed by a tunnel of cypress trees. Whether the alignment was intentional or accidental remains a mystery, but the view, which captures three nations at once (Italy, the Sovereign Order of Malta, and Vatican City), is unforgettable.

#8 Hidden Masterpieces by The Greats – For Free!

It's no secret that artists such as Michelangelo and Caravaggio shaped and painted this town into a living breathing piece of art. In Rome, art is ubiquitous, and many of its artistic treasures can be admired without setting foot in a gallery.

Where to find them:

- **Church of San Pietro in Vincoli** – Home to Michelangelo's majestic Moses sculpture.

- **Palazzo Farnese** – Features Michelangelo's architectural work on the upper floor, visible from the piazza.
- **Church of Santa Maria sopra Minerva** – Houses Michelangelo's Risen Christ statue beside the main altar. These sites prove that some of Rome's greatest masterpieces are still hidden in plain sight.

#9 Quartiere Coppedè

One of Rome's most unusual neighborhoods, Quartiere Coppedè feels like a storybook come to life. Designed in the early 20th century by architect Gino Coppedè, this whimsical district blends Art Nouveau, Baroque, and Gothic influences into a surreal mix of turrets, mosaics, and frescoed facades. The centerpiece, Piazza Mincio, features the *Fontana delle Rane* (Fountain of the Frogs), where even The Beatles once took a midnight dip after a concert. It's an architectural fantasy unlike anything else in the city.

#10 The Orange Garden (Giardino degli Aranci)

Perched on the Aventine Hill, this peaceful garden offers one of the most romantic panoramas of Rome. Through a grove of fragrant orange trees, the terrace opens onto a breathtaking view of St. Peter's Basilica framed perfectly across the Tiber. It's especially magical at sunset, when the golden light washes over the city and musicians sometimes play nearby.

#11 The Aventine Rose Garden (Roseto Comunale)

Just below the Orange Garden, this tranquil rose garden blooms with over 1,000 varieties of roses from around the world. It's a breathtaking spot in spring, offering serenity and floral perfume with sweeping views of the Palatine Hill.

#12 The Mouth of Truth (La Bocca della Verità)

Tucked into the portico of the medieval Church of Santa Maria in Cosmedin, this ancient marble mask is said to bite the hand of anyone who lies. Legend has it that even Audrey Hepburn tested her honesty here in *Roman Holiday*. Whether you believe the myth or not, it's one of the city's most iconic and delightfully odd relics.

#13 The Capuchin Crypt (Santa Maria della Concezione dei Cappuccini)

One of the most eerie and fascinating sites in Rome, this crypt contains the bones of over 3,700 monks arranged into chandeliers, arches and floral patterns. "What you are now, we once were; what we are now, you shall be" reads the inscription. A chilling reminder of life's impermanence that has fascinated visitors for centuries.

#14 Testaccio Market

Away from the tourist crowds, this neighborhood food market is where locals shop for Rome's freshest produce, cheese, and pasta ingredients. You'll also find modern street food stalls serving truffle paninis, Roman-style pizza, and tiramisu on the go. It's the perfect place to taste authentic Rome without the crowds.

#15 The Jewish Ghetto (Il Ghetto Ebraico)

One of Rome's most historic yet underexplored neighborhoods, the Jewish Ghetto blends ancient ruins, Renaissance charm and a vibrant culinary heritage. Don't miss the Portico d'Ottavia ruins and the famed *carciofi alla giudia*, deep-fried artichokes, a centuries-old Roman-Jewish delicacy.

#16 Domus Aurea (Nero's Golden Palace)

Buried beneath a park near the Colosseum lies Emperor Nero's lavish palace, complete with frescoes, marble halls and domed rooms painted in gold leaf. Guided tours use virtual-reality headsets to recreate its original splendor, letting you step inside one of ancient Rome's most extravagant homes.

#17 Quartiere Garbatella

A charming, pastel-hued residential district built in the 1920s, Garbatella feels more like a small Italian village than a Roman suburb. Its courtyards, archways, and local trattorias make it one of the most photogenic and authentically Roman neighborhoods to wander.

#18 Palazzo Doria Pamphilj

Hidden just off the busy Via del Corso, Palazzo Doria Pamphilj is one of Rome's most exquisite private palaces and still home to the noble Doria Pamphilj family. Behind its unassuming façade lies a lavish 17th-century residence filled with grand salons, mirrored galleries, and one of the city's finest private art collections. Masterpieces by Velázquez, Caravaggio, Titian, and Raphael line the gilded halls, while the family's history is narrated through portraits, letters, and furnishings preserved for centuries. Quiet, opulent, and often overlooked, this palace offers a rare glimpse into the elegance of Rome's aristocratic past.

#19 Galleria Sciarra

Tucked between Via del Corso and Piazza Venezia, the Galleria Sciarra is one of Rome's true hidden gems. A dazzling courtyard that feels like stepping inside a painted jewel box. Built in the late 19th century as part of a noble family's palace, the gallery was designed in the Art Nouveau style and adorned with vibrant frescoes celebrating feminine virtue, beauty, and strength. Its glass-and-iron ceiling floods the space with light, illuminating every golden detail.

Today, the galleria remains open to the public during business hours, a peaceful escape from the crowds and a stunning example of Rome's elegant turn-of-the-century artistry.

#20 Villa Medici

Perched on the Pincio Hill near the top of the Spanish Steps, Villa Medici is one of Rome's most refined Renaissance villas, surrounded by manicured gardens and commanding panoramic views of the city. Built in the 16th century for Cardinal Ferdinando de' Medici, the villa later became home to the French  Academy in Rome, a center for art, music, and scholarship that continues to host resident artists to this day. Visitors can stroll through the serene gardens, admire ancient statues, and explore the elegant interiors where centuries of creativity and diplomacy have intertwined.

#21 Palazzo Altemps

Located just steps from Piazza Navona, Palazzo Altemps is one of Rome's most elegant Renaissance palaces and part of the National Roman Museum. Built in the 15th century for the noble Riario family and later acquired by Cardinal Altemps, the palace beautifully combines classical grandeur with refined intimacy. Its frescoed ceilings and graceful courtyards provide the perfect setting for an extraordinary collection of ancient Greek and Roman sculptures, many once owned by aristocratic families. Highlights include mythological masterpieces like the Ludovisi Ares and the Suicidal Gaul. Quiet and uncrowded, Palazzo Altemps offers a serene and sophisticated journey through antiquity in the heart of the city.

#22 Basilica di Santo Stefano Rotondo al Celio

One of Rome's most unusual and ancient churches, the Basilica di Santo Stefano Rotondo stands on the Caelian Hill and dates back to the 5th century. Unique for its perfectly circular design inspired by early Christian martyria, the basilica was dedicated to Saint Stephen, the first Christian martyr. Inside, a ring of marble columns encircles the altar, while striking Renaissance frescoes depict scenes of martyrdom — both haunting and historically significant. Despite its quiet setting, far from the city's usual crowds, Santo Stefano Rotondo offers one of the most powerful glimpses into early Christian architecture and devotion in Rome.

#23 Largo di Torre Argentina

In the heart of Rome's historic center lies Largo di Torre Argentina, an open-air archaeological site that reveals four ancient Roman temples and part of Pompey's Theatre, the very spot where Julius Caesar was assassinated in 44 BC. The sunken ruins, discovered by chance during construction in the 1920s, now sit below modern street level, offering a striking glimpse into layers of Rome's past. Today, the site is also famous for its feline residents. A cat sanctuary occupies part of the ruins, caring for hundreds of strays that lounge among the columns and stones of history. It's one of Rome's most unexpected and quietly captivating corners.

#24 Oratorio del Santissimo Crocifisso

Hidden near Piazza Venezia, the Oratorio del Santissimo Crocifisso is one of Rome's most intimate artistic and spiritual treasures. Closely tied to the nearby Church of San Marcello al Corso, the oratory was built in the 16th century by the Confraternity of the Most Holy Crucifix, a brotherhood founded after a remarkable event. When San Marcello was destroyed by fire in 1519, only a wooden crucifix survived. Three years later, this same cross was carried through the streets during a plague outbreak and, according to tradition, brought the epidemic to an end.

In gratitude, the brotherhood constructed the oratory as a place of worship and service to the poor, enshrining the miraculous crucifix within. The interior, a jewel of Counter-Reformation art, glows with frescoes by Federico Zuccari and other masters, depicting scenes from the Passion in vivid color and emotion. Quiet, reverent, and steeped in history, the Oratorio del Santissimo Crocifisso remains a powerful reminder of faith, art, and compassion enduring through centuries.

#25 Parco degli Acquedotti

Stretching across the southeastern edge of Rome, Parco degli Acquedotti is a breathtaking park where ancient engineering and open countryside meet. Named for the towering aqueducts that once supplied water to the Eternal City, the park preserves massive stone arches from the *Aqua Claudia* and *Aqua Felix*, two of Rome's most impressive ancient aqueducts. Built nearly 2,000 years ago, their silhouettes still march across the fields like sleeping giants. The park's wide meadows, cypress trees, and distant views of the Apennines make it a favorite escape for locals, joggers, and photographers seeking Rome's quieter side. Especially at sunset, when golden light floods the arches, Parco degli Acquedotti feels like stepping into a timeless landscape where history and nature flow together.

#26 Teatro di Marcello & Portico of Octavia

Just a short walk from the Jewish Ghetto, the Teatro di Marcello is one of Rome's most fascinating ancient landmarks, often mistaken for a miniature Colosseum. Commissioned by Julius Caesar and completed by Emperor Augustus in 13 BC, the theater once held up to 20,000 spectators for plays and musical performances. Its tiered arches, later incorporated into a Renaissance palace, show how Rome has layered its history one era atop another. Nearby stands the Portico of Octavia, a colonnaded gateway built by Augustus in honor of his sister. Once the entrance to a grand complex of temples and libraries, it now frames the modern streets like an elegant ruin. Together, these two sites capture the essence of Rome. A city where ancient stones still pulse with life and memory.

#27 Villa Farnesina

Nestled in the charming Trastevere district, Villa Farnesina is one of Rome's most graceful Renaissance villas, built in the early 1500s for the wealthy banker Agostino Chigi. Designed by architect Baldassare Peruzzi, the villa embodies the harmony and refinement of High Renaissance art. A retreat where myth, beauty, and intellect intertwined. Inside, visitors can admire exquisite frescoes by Raphael and his pupils, including the famous *Triumph of Galatea*, as well as Peruzzi's illusionistic ceilings that blur the line between architecture and painting. Surrounded by peaceful gardens along the Tiber, Villa Farnesina offers a serene escape into the world of Renaissance splendor and imagination.

#28 St. Ivo alla Sapienza

Tucked behind an unassuming courtyard near Piazza Navona, St. Ivo alla Sapienza (*Sant'Ivo alla Sapienza*) is one of Rome's architectural masterpieces — a triumph of Baroque ingenuity designed by Francesco Borromini in the 17th century. Built as the chapel for the University of Rome (*La Sapienza*), it's renowned for its unique geometry: an interlocking star-shaped floor plan crowned by a spiraling lantern that seems to reach toward heaven. The church's harmonious curves and light-filled interior reflect Borromini's genius for combining mathematics, symbolism, and spiritual vision. Though less visited than the city's larger basilicas, St. Ivo alla Sapienza offers one of the most captivating architectural experiences in Rome. A perfect balance of intellect and grace.

#29 Trajan's Market

Often called the world's first shopping mall, Trajan's Market is one of ancient Rome's most fascinating and best-preserved architectural complexes. Built in the early 2nd century AD under Emperor Trajan, it once housed more than 150 shops, offices, and administrative spaces arranged along multiple terraces carved into the Quirinal Hill. The sweeping semicircular structure of red brick and marble showcases the engineering brilliance of the Romans, with vaulted halls and corridors that still feel remarkably modern. Today, visitors can explore its upper levels and the Museum of the Imperial Fora, which brings to life the grandeur of ancient commerce and civic life. Overlooking the Forum of Trajan, the market remains a powerful reminder that even in antiquity, Rome was a city built for both trade and spectacle.

#30 Temple of Hadrian (Tempio di Adriano)

Standing in Piazza di Pietra near the Pantheon, the Temple of Hadrian is one of the most elegant reminders of imperial Rome nestled within

the modern city. Built in AD 145 by Emperor Antoninus Pius in honor of his adoptive father Hadrian, the temple once dominated an entire forum. Eleven of its towering Corinthian columns still survive, seamlessly incorporated into a later 17th-century palace that now houses the Chamber of Commerce. At night, subtle lighting reveals the full majesty of the ancient stonework, creating one of the city's most atmospheric sights. Blending antiquity with everyday life, the Temple of Hadrian perfectly captures Rome's timeless rhythm, where ancient grandeur stands quietly among cafés and shops.

Museums

Rome's museums are time capsules of art, power, and imagination. From ancient marble halls to gilded Renaissance palaces. Whether you're drawn to classical sculpture, Baroque masterpieces, or contemporary creativity, the city offers a museum for every mood. Here are the collections no visitor should miss.

Capitoline Museums (Musei Capitolini)

Perched atop the Capitoline Hill and redesigned by Michelangelo, the Capitoline Museums form the world's oldest public art collection. Inside, you'll find masterpieces of classical sculpture such as the Capitoline Wolf, Dying Gaul, and Capitoline Venus, alongside paintings by Caravaggio and Titian. The museum's terrace also offers one of the most breathtaking views over the Roman Forum.

Galleria Borghese

Set within the lush Villa Borghese Gardens, the Galleria Borghese is an intimate museum showcasing some of Rome's most dazzling works of art. Bernini's sculptures including *Apollo and Daphne* and *The Rape of Proserpina* seem almost alive, while paintings by Caravaggio, Raphael, and Titian line the walls. Advance reservations are required, but the experience is worth every moment.

Galleria Doria Pamphilj

A hidden gem on Via del Corso, the Galleria Doria Pamphilj occupies a magnificent 17th-century palace still owned by the noble Doria Pamphilj family. The private collection includes works by Velázquez, Caravaggio, Raphael, and Titian, displayed in lavish rooms where chandeliers, mirrors, and gilded ceilings create a setting as spectacular as the art itself.

Palazzo Altemps

Part of the National Roman Museum, Palazzo Altemps offers a serene exploration of Greek and Roman sculpture within a Renaissance palace near Piazza Navona. Highlights include mythological masterpieces such as the *Ludovisi Ares* and the *Suicidal Gaul*, displayed as they once were in the private collections of noble families.

Palazzo Massimo alle Terme

Just steps from Termini Station, Palazzo Massimo is another branch of the National Roman Museum and a must-visit for lovers of classical art. Its frescoes, mosaics, and ancient jewelry capture the daily life and luxury of Imperial Rome, while the *Sleeping Hermaphroditus* and *Discobolus* rank among the city's most exquisite sculptures.

MAXXI – National Museum of 21st Century Arts

Designed by architect Zaha Hadid, MAXXI is Rome's bold leap into the contemporary. This dynamic museum showcases modern Italian and international art, photography, and architecture in fluid, futuristic spaces. It's a striking contrast to the city's ancient stones. Proof that Rome's creativity didn't end with the Renaissance.

Museo Nazionale Romano – Baths of Diocletian

Housed within the remains of the vast Baths of Diocletian, this branch of the National Roman Museum seamlessly blends ancient grandeur with archaeological insight. Built in the 3rd century AD, the complex once accommodated thousands of bathers daily. Today, its soaring halls and courtyards display inscriptions, sculptures, and artifacts that trace Rome's transformation from empire to empire. Michelangelo himself reimagined parts of the site when it was later converted into the Basilica of St. Mary of the Angels, adding a Renaissance touch to ancient stone.

Centrale Montemartini

Few places capture the contrast between past and present as vividly as Centrale Montemartini, an early-20th-century power station transformed into a museum. Here, ancient Roman statues stand among massive turbines, boilers, and steel machinery, creating a stunning dialogue between classical art and industrial design. Once an overflow gallery for the Capitoline Museums, it has become a destination in its own right. A place where marble gods gleam beneath factory lights, proving that Rome's art can find new life in any setting.

Museo dell'Ara Pacis

Along the banks of the Tiber, the Museo dell'Ara Pacis showcases one of the most beautiful monuments of Imperial Rome, the *Ara Pacis Augustae*, or "Altar of Peace." Commissioned by Emperor Augustus in 13 BC to celebrate the peace and prosperity of his reign, the marble altar is covered in exquisitely carved reliefs depicting mythological and ceremonial scenes. Its modern glass pavilion, designed by architect Richard Meier, contrasts strikingly with the ancient sculpture inside, creating a serene space where light, art, and history meet. The museum also includes exhibits on Augustus and the transformation of Rome during his rule, making it a must-see for lovers of classical art and design.

Pro Tips for Visiting Rome's Museums

• **Plan ahead:** The Galleria Borghese requires advance reservations, often several days ahead, while the Vatican Museums are best booked online to skip the long entry lines.

• **Timing matters:** Arrive early at major sites like the Vatican Museums and Capitoline Museums to enjoy quieter galleries before tour groups arrive. For a tranquil afternoon, visit Palazzo Altemps or Centrale Montemartini, both remain blissfully uncrowded.

• **Perfect pairings:** Combine the Capitoline Museums with nearby Piazza del Campidoglio and the Roman Forum for a deep dive into ancient history. Pair the Galleria Borghese with a stroll through Villa Borghese Gardens, or the Museo dell'Ara Pacis with a sunset walk along the Tiber.

• **Dress comfortably:** Expect marble floors and long gallery walks. Comfortable shoes are essential. Bring a light wrap or jacket; museum interiors can be cool, even in summer.

• **Hidden highlights:** Don't miss the Palazzo Massimo's ancient frescoes from Livia's villa, or the Ara Pacis's intricate carvings under the museum's glass canopy. Both are quiet masterpieces that reward a slower look.

• **When to go:** Museums are generally less crowded on weekday mornings and after 3 p.m. Avoid the first Sunday of each month unless you don't mind the crowds, that's when most state museums offer free entry.

Best Restaurants

Gourmet Dining in Rome: From Michelin Stars to Roman Classics

Rome's culinary scene is as layered and captivating as its history. A city where ancient recipes meet avant-garde artistry, and every meal tells a story. From candlelit terraces overlooking the Colosseum to family-run trattorias tucked down cobbled alleys, dining in the Eternal City is an experience of both indulgence and authenticity. Michelin-starred chefs reinterpret tradition with daring precision, while humble osterias continue to serve the soulful dishes that have defined Roman cooking for centuries. Whether you're savoring truffle-laced pasta beneath a frescoed ceiling or grabbing a crisp slice of pizza al taglio on the go, Rome proves that food here isn't just nourishment, it's culture, craftsmanship and pure passion on a plate.

Michelin-Starred Icons

La Pergola

Tucked high above Rome in the Rome Cavalieri Waldorf Astoria, La Pergola is the city's only three-Michelin-star restaurant. Under Chef Heinz Beck, Italian-Mediterranean cuisine meets museum-level refinement: delicate pasta dishes, a 2,500-label wine list, and sweeping city views that make dinner feel like an event.

Il Pagliaccio

Two Michelin stars for creativity: located near the Tiber, the kitchen of Anthony Genovese blends Italian traditions with Asian inflections, delivering a tasting menu that surprises at every turn.

Acquolina

Also rated two stars, this contemporary seafood-led fine dining spot at The First Roma near Piazza del Popolo offers modern design, a Mediterranean mood, and memorable dishes for the polished diner.

Enoteca La Torre

Sitting in the elegant Hotel Villa Laetitia, this two-star restaurant brings Campania influences, refined execution, and a top-tier wine cellar, ideal for a special-occasion night.

Aroma

With one Michelin star and a roof-top terrace facing the Colosseum, Aroma is an unforgettable pairing of view and haute Roman cuisine.

Pipero Roma

One star; located on Corso Vittorio Emanuele II, this stylish spot merges modern techniques with regional ingredients and offers a chic yet approachable fine-dining experience.

Imàgo

Sitting atop the Spanish Steps within the Hassler Hotel, this one-star restaurant pairs sweeping city views with elegant Italian dishes — perfect for a luxurious evening.

Per Me Giulio Terrinoni

Nestled near Via Giulia, this intimate one-star restaurant emphasizes sustainability, seasonal ingredients, and quiet elegance — a refined gem away from the buzz.

Glass Hostaria

Located in Trastevere, one star, modern design and a menu that re-imagines Italian classics with bold presentation, ideal if you want Michelin calibre in a vibrant neighbourhood.

Achilli al Parlamento

One star; a historic wine-bar-turned-fine-dining near the Italian Parliament. Traditional Campania roots meet upscale execution, one of Rome's freshest starred dining experiences.

Roman Classics You Must Eat

Spaghetti alla carbonara – Creamy, peppery, pork-rich: every Roman trattoria does it, but the city's best serve it simply, boldly, without fuss.

Cacio e pepe – Pecorino, cracked pepper, al dente pasta: this minimalist Roman masterpiece defines the local cuisine.

Supplì – Fried rice-balls stuffed with tomato and mozzarella, perfect for a snack or aperitivo stop between sights.

Carciofi alla giudia – Deep-fried Jewish-style artichokes from Rome's Ghetto: crisp leaves, nutty flavour, seasonal must-have.

Roman "fifth quarter" dishes (quinto quarto) – For the bold: tripe, oxtail stew (coda alla vaccinara), sweetbreads, and more — found in the city's oldest trattorias and emblematic of Roman food culture.

Recommended Non-Star Trattorias & Local Favorites

Trattoria Da Enzo al 29 (Trastevere) – A cozy, authentic spot for Roman classics like carbonara and cacio e pepe in a lively neighborhood setting.

Salumeria Roscioli / Roscioli (near Campo de' Fiori) – More than a deli: a full restaurant with traditional Roman dishes, excellent charcuterie, and wine by the glass. Beloved by locals.

Osteria Al Vicolo 9 (Monti) – Hidden away in Monti, this lively osteria offers generous menus, friendly chaos, and dishes like tripe done right.

Trapizzino (Trastevere) – Casual, fast, local: triangle-shaped bread pockets stuffed with classic Roman fillings. Perfect lunch stop.

Il Duca (Trastevere) – Homely atmosphere, excellent homemade pasta (especially truffle ravioli), and a true local feel in the heart of Trastevere.

Top Ten Bloggers' Recommendations

#1 Pianostrada Laboratorio di Cucina

The all-female team prepares delicious panini, inventive salads, pastas, and homemade desserts.

The all-female Pianostrada team just relocated from their tiny Trastevere facility to their new, bigger space over the river, equipped with a lovely indoor garden and a wide open kitchen. Freshly baked bread and foccacia are used to produce outstanding sandwiches (such as the iconic salt cod burger served in a squid-ink bun), and there are inventive salads, pastas, and secondi, as well as home-made pastries and cakes.

#2 Osteria Fernanda

Osteria Fernanda ranks with several of the city's most recognized restaurants. The cuisine is quite avant-garde, with dishes that are both "comfort food" and creative culinary experiences: seek for the rigatoni with a sweet roots-based sauce and the snails and eel with radishes and Campari. The comprehensive wine list includes renowned champagnes to wash down the equally wonderful treats.

#3 Marigold

This micro-bakery, café-restaurant brings together the best of Italian seasonal cuisine and minimalist Scandinavian design. The menu changes daily and features fresh, foraged ingredients prepared in creative ways like stracciatella with artichokes and zucchini with cardoncelli mushrooms and walnut pesto. Stop by on weekends for brunch, which includes avocado toast with poached eggs and fresh cinnamon swirls.

#4 Coromandel

Coromandel, with its colorful furnishings and clever design elements, is one of the coziest restaurants to visit on rainy days and chilly evenings. It has an Alice in Wonderland vibe and delivers the greatest brunch in town, with a tempting selection of pancakes, eggs, pastries, and coffee delights. It's also a good option for lunch and supper, with meals like roast suckling pig with bok cabbage and a sweet-and-sour onions sauce or scallop tartare with passion fruit and bacon. The outstanding soufflè with vanilla and Armagnac cream is not to be missed.

#5 Enoteca La Torre

Enoteca La Torre, located within Anna Venturini Fendi's exquisite Villa Laetitia, reflects the essence of la dolce vita. This high-end restaurant provides beautiful meals that suit its stately setting: led by Domenico Stile, a Campania native, the menu features Southern Italian delicacies such as buffalo milk cheeses, Sorrento lemons, and fresh seafood. Choose the chef's seven-course surprise tasting menu for a wonderful treat.

#6 Guilia

Giulia, a romantic restaurant on one of Rome's most exquisite avenues, offers flavor and flare to the heart of the Eternal City. Chef Pierluigi Gallo, who hails from Campania and trained in Abruzzo, reimagines classic comfort food that will please customers. The oxtail is served with celery and chocolate ketchup, while the spaghetti is topped with a crimson sauce prepared from baby octopus, sea snails, and sea urchins.

#7 Va. Do

Va.Do is a restaurant with a modern, industrial style and an extensive cuisine to satisfy all tastes. Even when sampling cosmopolitan delicacies such couscous with tofu, chicken curry, ravioli with hog cheek, and tuna tartare, fish lovers, meat eaters, and vegetarians will feel at home. If you're yearning Roman classics, don't worry: you'll find them here, as well as sweets like tiramisu, almond-flour chocolate cake, and frozen delicacies.

#8 Trattoria Pennestri

Trattoria Pennestri, with its cozy décor and courteous service, is the type of place that welcomes you to stay and enjoy a leisurely lunch with excellent company. The food, like the atmosphere, is rustic but polished, with a handpicked selection of innovative dishes that make the most of seasonal ingredients. The wine list is also excellent, with a large range available by the glass. Save space for one of the city's greatest desserts: a sweet and salty chocolate mousse flavored with rosemary and served on Sardinian flatbread.

#9 Trapizzino

Stefano Callegari, the genius of Trapizzino, created this revolutionary street cuisine after working as a pizza delivery guy in 2008. Following that, he enrolled in a culinary training program and started a string of well-known pizzerias and street food outlets. The trapizzino is a soft and mouthwateringly flavorful focaccia pouch filled with deliciousness ranging from eggplant parmesan to meatballs with tomato sauce and chicken cacciatore, as well as vegetarian options like Roman artichoke and misticanza – a mixture of leafy greens sautéed in garlic and red chili pepper.

#10 Da Enzo al 29

Da Enzo, a lovely small café nestled on a quiet lane in Trastevere, is one of Rome's more distinctive trattorias, drawing a throng for its basic, honest cooking and handful of outdoor tables. Eating here seems like a family reunion, with generous quantities that are beautifully cooked. You can't go wrong with anything on the menu, from carbonara and meatballs to braised artichokes and tiramisu, but get there early or expect a long wait.

Worst Restaurants

Rome may be one of the greatest food cities in the world, but even here, the occasional misstep can leave you with a bitter taste and a lighter wallet. With its endless stream of tourists and postcard-perfect piazzas, the city is home to a handful of restaurants that prioritize foot traffic over flavor, and profit over pride. These aren't the places locals frequent or where culinary tradition thrives, they're the ones serving reheated carbonara under heat lamps, marking up basic wines, or charging you for bread you didn't ask for. Whether it's dishonest billing, microwaved meals, or bland dishes disguised by stunning views, these are the restaurants that leave travelers wishing they'd walked just a few more blocks. Rome deserves better and so do you.

Baccano

Steps from the Trevi Fountain, Baccano draws in passersby with its sleek Parisian brasserie décor and promise of fine dining. But the experience often fails to live up to the setting. Diners report slow service, overpriced pasta, and a general lack of hospitality that feels more transactional than Italian. Reviews cite forty-five-minute waits for mediocre dishes and automatic bread charges added to the bill. Despite its prime location and chic ambience, Baccano has become a cautionary tale of style over substance. One of those places that looks the part but forgets the heart of Roman hospitality: warmth, simplicity, and soul.

Vino e Focaccia

Few places have earned the kind of warnings that shadow Vino e Focaccia. Multiple travelers have accused the restaurant of doubling prices between what's listed on the menu and what's printed on the final bill. One reviewer on a Rick Steves forum called it a "horrible scam restaurant," noting that the staff removed the receipt before it could be photographed. Dish quality takes a back seat to aggressive pricing tactics, making this spot feel more like a trap than a trattoria. Until transparency and trust are restored, Vino e Focaccia is best left off your itinerary.

Landmark-Area Tourist Traps

It's not one name, but a pattern. Restaurants clustered directly around landmarks like the Trevi Fountain, Spanish Steps, and Piazza Navona are often the worst offenders when it comes to inflated prices and uninspired food. You'll recognize them by the oversized laminated menus with photos, staff waving you in from the sidewalk, and mile-long lists of dishes that try to cater to every palate. From sushi to schnitzel to spaghetti. Inside, the food is often cold, flavorless, or poorly executed, and it's not uncommon to be charged for things you never ordered: a mystery "service fee," a bread basket, or bottled water you never touched. These restaurants thrive on convenience, not quality, and offer the kind of meal you'll quickly regret in a city where extraordinary dining is around every corner.

Antico Caffè di Marte (Rome)

Located near central tourist zones, this restaurant made headlines after a group of diners were charged over €400 for two plates of spaghetti with fish and two glasses of water.

Multiple reviews and travel forums describe the billing as misleading: fish priced per 100 g turned into multiple kilograms, and extra service/tip charges were added without clear disclosure.

S.P.Q.R. Restaurant (Via di Tor Millina, just off Piazza Navona, Rome)

Found via a long-running complaint thread on TripAdvisor, this restaurant has been flagged for "…handing diners a different menu than the one they ordered from, then charging higher prices."

Though less sensational than Antico Caffè di Marte, the consistent pattern of menu-trickery and tourist-targeting makes it valid for inclusion in the "to-avoid" list.

Trattoria Antonio (Via della Maddalena)

Near the Pantheon. Multiple reports of inflated bills and a €16 charge for "table service" even when ordering basic items.

Caffè Vaticano (Viale Vaticano)

Located just outside the Vatican Museums. Known for poor service, cold food, and shockingly high prices — like €8 for a Coke and €20+ for a basic salad.

Ristorante Naumachia (Via Celimontana)

Near the Colosseum. Tourists report being charged "accidentally" for extra items they never ordered. Food is overpriced and underwhelming.

Ristorante Tre Pupazzi (Via dei Tre Pupazzi)

Tourist trap near the Vatican. Reports include being charged for items not ordered, rude staff, and watered-down wine.

Ristorante Il Bocconcino (Via Ostilia)

Colosseum adjacent. Frequent complaints of bad food, long waits, and unexpected service fees. Known among locals as a "no-go" zone.

Caffè Domiziano (Piazza Navona)

Another gorgeous location with disappointing results. Guests have complained of overpriced cold pizza, salty pasta, and refusal to provide receipts.

Travel-Savvy Tips: How to Avoid Tourist Trap Restaurants

- **Look for authentic indicators**: Shorter menus, more Italian than English spoken, fewer photo-menus outside.
- **Avoid the lure of the landmark view**: Some of the best meals are two or three blocks away from the tourist hotspots.
- **Beware of aggressive staff outside**: If someone is waving you in on the street or offering "special deals," that's usually a red flag.
- **Check the check**: Be sure you know what you're being charged for (bread basket, service, bottled water). If the bill surprises you, speak up.
- **Trust your local radar**: If it looks like every other tourist is eating somewhere else and mostly locals are absent, that's telling.
- **Read recent reviews**: Quality can change quickly. A restaurant praised two years ago might have slipped.
- **Walk away if in doubt**: There are hundreds of restaurants in Rome, if something feels off, it's worth moving on for better.

Best Hotels

Rome isn't just a city, it's an immersion. And where you rest your head at night should feel just as cinematic as your days wandering its ancient streets. Whether you're sipping prosecco on a rooftop terrace with the Colosseum glowing in the distance or tucking into a quiet boutique hotel near cobblestone alleyways, Rome offers accommodations that blend luxury, history, and heart. From five-star stunners that once housed nobility to sleek mid-range stays with design-forward flair, to humble hidden gems that don't skimp on soul, here are the top places to stay in the Eternal City, no matter your travel style or budget.

Luxe Roman Retreats

Hotel de Russie

An iconic sanctuary between the Spanish Steps and Piazza del Popolo, Hotel de Russie marries classic Roman charm with modern sophistication. Its lush secret garden, elegant spa, and sleek rooms make it a favorite of celebrities and discerning travelers alike. The Stravinskij Bar's aperitivo scene is worth checking in for alone.

The Hassler Roma

Perched atop the Spanish Steps like a crown jewel, the Hassler is a symbol of timeless elegance. With panoramic views, old-world service, and interiors that evoke a bygone era of grandeur, it's a favorite for honeymoons, high-profile stays, and anyone craving five-star nostalgia with impeccable polish.

Palazzo Manfredi – Relais & Châteaux

If waking up to the Colosseum outside your window sounds like a dream, this boutique five-star delivers. Blending contemporary luxury with ancient proximity, Palazzo Manfredi offers Michelin-star dining at Aroma and an experience as unforgettable as Rome itself.

Mid-Range Marvels

Nerva Boutique Hotel

Tucked beside the Roman Forum, Nerva blends boutique style with cozy intimacy. Expect curated decor, warm service, and a location that puts history quite literally at your doorstep. Ideal for couples and solo travelers seeking thoughtful touches without the five-star splurge.

Hotel Smeraldo

Just steps from Campo de' Fiori, this polished three-star offers clean rooms, a breezy rooftop bar, and a price point that makes staying central surprisingly attainable. It's simple, safe and always dependable. A favorite for repeat visitors who know what matters.

Hotel Artemide

Set in a 19th-century building on Via Nazionale, Artemide punches above its weight with luxe linens, a rooftop restaurant, and a spa that rivals higher-priced stays. Service is standout, and rooms are soundproofed. a rare win in the heart of the city.

Budget Gems That Don't Feel Cheap

The Hive Hotel

Bright, modern, and surprisingly stylish, The Hive offers large rooms with minimalist flair and a rooftop bar that feels anything but budget. Located near Termini Station, it's ideal for travelers looking for a convenient, upbeat home base.

Hotel Golden

Family-run and full of heart, Hotel Golden is a beloved choice for travelers who want warmth over flash. Rooms are basic but spotless, and the owners go out of their way to offer advice, directions, and a genuine Roman welcome.

Hotel Canada, BW Premier Collection

Classic decor, spacious rooms, and a central location make this Best Western a smart choice for families or solo travelers. It feels more boutique than brand, and with easy access to transport, it's a practical pick that doesn't compromise comfort.

Best Time to Visit

Rome's best travel months (also busiest and most expensive) are April, May, June, September, October, and early November. These months combine the convenience of peak season with pleasant weather.

Spring

Best time to explore the city's beauty

Spring is a fantastic season to visit Rome. The weather is ideal, generally warm enough to dine outside, and the city is stunning with beautiful skies and spring flowers.

Take in the Spanish Steps, which are decked with hundreds of vases of flowering, vividly colored azaleas from early April until mid-May. The Spanish Steps (Scalinata della Trinità dei Monti), which have drawn visitors since the 18th century, are an excellent place to people-watch. From Piazza di Spagna, 135 glittering stairs lead to the iconic Chiesa della Trinità dei Monti. The Chiesa della Trinità dei Monti, located at the top of the stairs, is known for the spectacular views of Rome from its front stairway, as well as its stunning murals by Daniele da Volterra. The "sinking boat" fountain, the Barcaccia, can be seen on the piazza. However, be careful of new restrictions prohibiting "camping" or "sitting out" on the stairs.

Summer

Best time for festivals

Summer kicks off with plenty of festivals, and is considered one of the more busy times for tourists.

In June, Estate Romana begins. This big summer festival, which runs from June to September, involves everything from concerts and dance performances to book fairs, puppet shows and late-night museum openings.

Also beginning in June is Lungo il Tevere, a summer-long festival with live music, film screenings, exhibitions, craft stalls and bars, all on the banks of the Tiber between Ponte Sublicio and Ponte Sisto.

Fall

Best time for theater

After the August slumber, life returns to the metropolis. The kids return to school, and residents return to work, but there's still a laid-back summer attitude, and the weather is perfect. However, keep in mind that high-season charges still apply.

Romaeuropa, Rome's fall festival of theater, opera, and dance, is one of the month's most important events. From mid-September to mid-November, events span from avant-garde dance to installations, multimedia presentations, recitals, and readings.

In late October, Rome's film festival, Festa del Cinema di Roma, lays out the red carpet for Hollywood A-listers and Italian film industry heavyweights. The event is hosted in the Parco della Musica Auditorium.

Winter

Best time for shopping

Rates are at their lowest from November through March, with the exception of Christmas and New Year's. Winter fashion deals begin in January, making it an excellent time to go shopping. Sports lovers may also enjoy the Six Nations rugby competition in February.

Best Things to do in Rome, Month-by-Month

Here's a monthly breakdown of what to anticipate in Rome throughout the year. Every event is subject to change.

January

The winter chill sets in as the New Year's celebrations wane. The winter bargains are a wonderful distraction at this calm time of year.

Winter fashion sales are important occasions.

February

Colorful carnival festivities and weekend invasions by joyful rugby supporters in town for the annual Six Nations rugby tournament disrupt Rome's winter peace.

Carnevale, the Six Nations rugby competition, and parades at Piazza del Popolo, Via del Corso, Piazza di Spagna, and Piazza Navona are all important events.

March

Spring brings with it blossoming flowers, increasing temperatures, and unexpected showers. Unless Easter happens in late March, the city is rather quiet, and low-season pricing remain in effect.

Important dates: Giornate FAI di Primavera.

April

April in Rome is characterized by beautiful, bright weather, ardent Easter celebrations, and azaleas on the Spanish Steps. Expect peak-season pricing.

Key events include the Natale di Roma, the Maratona di Roma, Easter festivities, and the azaleas on the Spanish Steps.

May

May is a busy, peak-season month, owing to the nicer weather.

Key events include the Primo Maggio and the Internazionale BNL d'Italia.

June

Summer has here, bringing scorching weather and Italian school vacations. The city's festival season kicks off with a slew of outdoor activities.

Festa dei Santi Pietro e Paolo, Isola del Cinema (mid-June to September), Lungo il Tevere, Roma Incontro il Mondo (late June to August), Estate Romana (late June to August) (June to September).

July

Summer temperatures make touring a physical exercise, but come dark, the city's streets come alive with inhabitants out to enjoy the summer festivities.

Festa de' Noantri, the summer season of music and ballet at the Teatro dell'Opera, and the Concerti del Tempietto.

August

As inhabitants abandon the city for their summer vacations, Rome melts in the heat. Many businesses close around August 15, however hoteliers provide discounts and there are several summer activities to attend.

Festa della Madonna della Neve, Ferragosto are important dates.

September

In September, kids return to school and residents return to work, but the weather remains pleasant. High-season pricing is still in effect.

Important dates: Romaeuropa

October

Autumn is a nice time to come since the weather is still pleasant, Romaeuropa offers plenty of cultural activities, and there are less visitors about because schools have returned.

Festa del Cinema di Roma is a major event.

November

Despite being the wettest month, November offers many advantages: low-season costs, market stalls brimming with abundant fall vegetables, and no lines outside the major attractions. It's a rather calm time of year in terms of events.

Key events include the Roma Jazz Festival and the Festival Internazionale di Musica e Arte Sacra.

December

The build-up to Christmas is a joyous period. The Christmas lights are turned on, shopping becomes more urgent, and presepi (nativity scenes) arise around town, most notably in St Peter's Square.

Piazza Navona Christmas Fair is a major event.

4 Days in Rome Travel Itinerary

Day 1

Colosseum of Rome, Palatine Hill, Roman Forum, Knights of Malta Keyhole, Trastevere

Day 2

Vatican Museums, Castel Sant'Angelo

Day 3

St. Peter's Basilica, Pantheon, Doria Pamphilj Gallery, Altare della Patria, Piazza Navona

Day 4

Galleria Borghese, Spanish Steps, Trevi Fountain, Basilica of Santa Maria Maggiore

4-Day Travel Itinerary

Rome wasn't built in a day and you won't see it all in four. But with the right itinerary, you can soak in the grandeur, chaos, flavor, and magic of the Eternal City without feeling rushed. This four-day guide balances iconic landmarks with hidden gems, mouthwatering meals with leisurely piazza moments, and ancient ruins with modern-day dolce vita. Whether it's your first time in Rome or your fifth, these four days are designed to leave you breathless, full, and already plotting your return.

Day 1: Colosseum of Rome, Palatine Hill, Roman Forum, Knights of Malta Keyhole, Trastevere

Morning

07:30 AM – 08:30 AM: Start your first day with a cup of coffee and a pastry at 081 Caffè or Antico Caffe Del Brasile.

Visit the Iconic Colosseum

08:30 AM – 10:00 AM: The Colosseum (Colosseo) is the world's biggest amphitheatre. In 72 AD, Emperor Vespasian commissioned its construction. The Colosseum was a gladiatorial arena that could hold up to 80,000 people. It was once flooded by the Romans for boat fights.

Many gladiators were killed here. More specifically, over 500,000 people and twice as many animals. The final gladiatorial combat occurred in 435 AD.

Explore Palatine Hill

10:00 AM – 12:00 PM: Palatine Hill (Palatino) is the city's historic core. It is, in reality, the birthplace of the Eternal City. Romulus and Remus, the founders of Rome, are said to have resided in a cave on Palatine Hill.

During Augustus' reign, the Palatine Hill was a prosperous community of rich Romans. The ruins of Augustus and Livia's imperial residence may still be seen.

There is a lot to see on Palatine Hill. You'll need more time than you did at the Colosseum. Also, remember to wear comfy shoes.

Lunch

12:00 PM – 02:00 PM: Lunch may be had at Fuorinorma or Mizio's Street Food. Fuorinorma is an excellent choice for a wine, cheese, and salami tray. Mizio's Street Food is a great place for a fast lunch and delicious sandwiches.

Afternoon

Stroll through the Roman Forum

02:00 PM – 03:00 PM: The Roman Forum (Foro Romano) was the beating heart of ancient Rome. It was the centre of the political and cultural life of the city. All the important monuments, temples and courthouses were located here.

Today, you can still see the ruins of the royal residence, Temple of Saturn, Temple of Vesta and many other significant buildings.

Keyhole of the Knights of Malta

03:20 PM – 03:40 PM: The Knights of Malta Keyhole gives one of the city's most unusual vistas. When you look through it, you'll notice the dome of St. Peter's perfectly centered.

The entrance in issue goes to the Knights of Malta Priory. As a result, the perspective depicts three countries at once: Italy, the Vatican, and Malta. The keyhole, on the other hand, is not marked in any manner. Simply search for a green door at the crossroads of via di S. Sabina and Porta Lavernale Street

Discover Trastevere

04:00 PM – 05:00 PM: Trastevere is the most picturesque district. Cobblestone streets, small markets and coffee shops, Roman trattorias, artisan workshops, it has it all. It's the perfect place to wander and get lost.

If you look for some delicious Roman food, this is the place to go. The area is full of small traditional restaurants and cafés, that serve mouth-watering food.

Dinner

Dinner at I Pizzicaroli Trastevere or La Tavernetta 29 da Tony e Andrea will round out the first day of the agenda. I Pizzicaroli Trastevere serves a lighter meal with a salami and cheese buffet. If you're looking for a fancy supper, La Tavernetta 29 da Tony e Andrea is the place to go.

Archbasilica of St. John Lateran

Archbasilica of St. John Lateran is the most important of the four papal major basilicas. In fact, it's the mother church of the Roman Catholic faithful. That's why it's called an archbasilica. St. John Lateran Archbasilica is also the oldest church in the whole of Europe.

Baths of Caracalla

Going to baths was an important part of the daily life of the Romans. It was a place to socialize, gossip and even discuss politics.

The Baths of Caracalla were the largest thermal baths in the world during the 3rd century. In fact, Terme di Caracalla was a spa complex, that includes also reading and exercising areas, gardens and restaurants.

Although today only ruins are left from this place, you can still feel its splendour.

Day 2: Vatican Museums, Castel Sant'Angelo

Morning

08:00 AM – 08:30 AM

Start your second day with a breakfast at Sciascia Caffè 1919 or Forno Feliziani.

Explore the Vatican Museums.

08:45 AM – 01:00 PM: Most visitors rush through the Vatican Museums like pilgrims in a daze. Eyes tilted skyward, necks craned toward the Sistine Chapel, cameras trailing behind Raphael's School of Athens. But linger a little longer, and the deeper treasures begin to emerge. The Gallery of Maps, for instance, isn't just cartography, it's a 16th-century flex of papal power and world-building, each fresco not just a region but a worldview. The ethnological museum, quietly tucked away, holds sacred objects gifted from across the globe: Zulu necklaces, Buddhist scrolls, Aztec statues, proof that Rome's spiritual empire was always reaching, absorbing, and interpreting the divine from every corner.

Then there's the modern religious art collection, where Van Gogh, Dalí, and Bacon brush against the sacred in unsettling, luminous ways. It's the Vatican as you've never seen it: honest, evolving, even raw. Walk the halls with reverence, yes, but also with curiosity. The real magic of the Vatican Museums isn't just what's on display, but what it reveals about power, perception, and the unrelenting human need to make the invisible visible.

Lunch

01:00 PM – 03:00 PM: Ristorante dei Musei serves some of the greatest pizza in town. The Loft is the place to go for a salami and cheese plate. Try the gelato at Lemongrass after lunch

Afternoon

Tour Castel Sant'Angelo

03:00 PM – 05:00 PM: The Roman emperor Hadrian built the castle as a mausoleum for his family in 123 AD. However, its purpose changed several times over the centuries.

During his reign, Emperor Aurelian transformed the mausoleum into a military fortress. He also incorporated it into the city walls. The purpose of the fortress was to defend the northern entrance of the Eternal City.

In the 13th century, a covered fortified corridor (called Passetto di Borgo) was constructed. The corridor connects Vatican City and the castle. You can take a glimpse of this secret corridor if you take the Angels and Demons tour.

From the beginning of the 14th century, the papacy took control of the fortress and converted it to a castle. Papal apartments were built to ensure a comfortable stay in case of a siege.

Taste some authentic Italian food

Finish the day with a dinner at Wine Bar De' Penitenzieri or La Fraschetta di Castel Sant'Angelo. Both restaurants serve authentic Italian food.

Day 3: St. Peter's Basilica, Pantheon, Doria Pamphilj Gallery, Altare della Patria, Piazza Navona

Morning

08:00 AM – 08:45 AM: Start the third day of the itinerary 4 days in Rome with some pastry and coffee at Bar Pasticceria Gelateria Parenti Silvano.

The Basilica of St. Peter and St. Peter's Square

09:00 AM – 11:30 AM: St. Peter's Basilica, located in Vatican City, is one of the world's biggest cathedrals. It is also one of the Eternal City's four great basilicas. Among them are St. John Lateran

Basilica, Santa Maria Maggiore, and St. Paul Outside the Walls. All four basilicas are extremely stunning, so if you have the time, go see them all.

St. Peter's Basilica was built on the burial location of Saint Peter, one of Jesus' twelve apostles.

The Pietà is one of the basilica's most iconic monuments. It is a marble sculpture representing Mary clutching her dead son's corpse after the crucifixion. The sculpture was produced by Michelangelo between 1499 and 1500. This work of art is now protected by bulletproof glass after a visitor vandalized it with a hammer in 1972.

Lunch

11:45 AM – 01:30 PM: Lunch may be had at Likeat or Pane Pane Vino Ar Vino. Both eateries serve delicious sandwiches.

Admire the Pantheon

01:30 PM – 02:00 PM: Continue this Rome sightseeing itinerary with a visit to the Pantheon. Pantheon is the best-preserved monument from ancient Rome. Its exact construction date is unknown, but it was around 126 AD.

The most fascinating feature of the Pantheon is its dome. It's the largest unsupported dome in the world! Nowadays, this former Roman temple serves as a church.

Be amazed by Doria Pamphilj Gallery

02:15 PM – 04:00 PM: Doria Pamphilj Gallery is housed in a gorgeous palace that dates back to the 16th century. The gallery features one of the richest private art collection in Rome. Even if you aren't into art, it's worth visiting to see the lavish state apartments. There is a free audio guide, that is narrated by Jonathan Pamphilj himself. Today, the Doria Pamphilj family still owns the palace.

View the magnificent Altare della Patria.

04:15 PM – 04:45 PM: The Altare della Patria, commonly known as the National Monument to Victor Emmanuel II, is one of Rome's most majestic structures. The Altare della Patria is a monument dedicated to Italy's first king, Victor Emmanuel.

Take the lift to the panoramic terrace for spectacular city views.

See the famous Piazza Navona

05:00 PM – 05:30 PM: Piazza Navona is a charming square and a popular meeting spot. It's surrounded by small restaurants and there are regularly street artists.

Dinner

Finish the day with a dinner at Mimì e Cocò or Osteria del Pegno.

Palazzo Colonna

Palazzo Colonna is an art gallery that exhibits works by prominent Italian and international painters from the 15th and 16th centuries. The aristocratic Colonna family still owns this stunning 14th-century mansion. Unfortunately, this lovely establishment is only open on Saturday mornings.

Capitoline Museums

Capitoline Museums are divided into two buildings: Palazzo dei Conservatori and Palazzo Nuovo. The majority of the collection comprises of statues, sculptures, and paintings by well-known painters like as Caravaggio, Rubens, and Tiziano. The original statue of the Capitoline Wolf, the city's emblem, may also be found here.

Day 4: Galleria Borghese, Spanish Steps, Trevi Fountain, Basilica of Santa Maria Maggiore

Morning

08:00 AM – 08:30 AM: Begin the final day of your four-night Rome vacation with breakfast at D'Angelo Caffè or Trecaffè.

Both coffee cafes serve delicious sandwiches and pastries.

Admire the art at Galleria Borghese

08:45 AM – 11:15 AM: Galleria Borghese is the noble Borghese family's vacation house. It is also a must-see for any art enthusiast. Its incredible collection includes masterpieces by Caravaggio and Bernini.

ah Melland

Spanish Steps

11:30 AM – 12:00 PM: Spanish Steps is one of the most city emblematic spots. The staircase connects Piazza di Spagna with Trinità dei Monti Church. The Spanish Steps are truly beautiful in late April when they are decorated with 300 white and lilac azalea plants.

12:00 PM – 02:00 PM: Stop for some tasty panini and salad at Ami Bistrot or Burro e Alici.

Toss a coin in Trevi Fountain

02:00 PM – 02:30 PM: Trevi Fountain (Fontana di Trevi) is the largest and most beautiful fountain in the city. It's a must-see when in Rome. And don't forget to throw out a coin over your shoulder in the fountain. This will ensure a return to the Eternal City.

Santa Maria Maggiore Basilica

02:50 PM – 03:30 PM: The Basilica of Santa Maria Maggiore is one of the Eternal City's four great basilicas. It's a really gorgeous fifth-century church. The basilica was erected on the site where, according to mythology, snow fell in the summer of 358 AD.

Dinner

Finish your four days in Rome with a meal at Ristorante Nerone or Colline Emiliane. Both are ideal places to spend your final evening in the Eternal City.

Learn how to make homemade pasta.

There is no better way to end your four days in Rome than by taking a pasta-making workshop. You'll prepare, eat, and learn the secrets of preparing pasta with a local chef.

Turn become a gladiator.

At a school in Rome, you may learn how to be a gladiator. Learn the fundamentals of sword fighting and discover more about the gladiators of ancient Rome.

Outside the Walls, St. Paul's Basilica

Outside the Walls Basilica is located a little outside of the city center. It is, nevertheless, well worth a visit! It's one of the four great basilicas, and it's breathtaking. It is a visual feast, with gilded mosaics and massive marble columns.

Farnesina Villa

With its stunning frescoes and ceilings, Villa Farnesina is a real masterpiece of the Italian Renaissance. It was erected in the 16th century for rich Sienese banker Agostino Chigi. The property, located in Trastevere, is a quiet refuge away from the hordes of visitors. Remember that Villa Farnesina is only open in the mornings.

Visit the ominous Capuchin Crypt.

The Capuchin Crypt is a genuinely one-of-a-kind and interesting location. When the Catholic order's monks arrived, they brought 300 cartloads of deceased friars with them. They did not, however, rebury the skeletons. They were used to embellish the walls of the crypt, which has six chapels. More than 4,000 skeletons were carved in mosaics. There are even mummified monks masquerading as friars!

Rome's Catacombs

The catacombs are a maze of underground corridors stretching for several kilometers. They were used for funerals from the second to the fifth centuries AD. Following that, the catacombs were abandoned and looted on a regular basis. There are about 60 catacombs, but only five are accessible to the public.

Budgeting for Rome

What amount of cash will you require for your vacation to Rome?

You should budget roughly €131 ($138) per day for your holiday in Rome, as this is the average daily price based on other guests' costs. Previous visitors spent an average of €37 ($39) on meals for one day and €17 ($18) on local transportation. In addition, the typical hotel room in Rome costs €134 ($142). So, a one-week vacation to Rome for two individuals costs on average €1,836 ($1,939). All of these typical travel rates were gathered from previous travelers to assist you in planning your own trip budget.

Accommodations Budget in Rome (Average Daily Costs)

In Rome, the average price for one person's lodging is €67. The average price for a hotel room in Rome for two persons sharing a regular double-occupancy hotel room is €134.

Transportation Budget in Rome (Average Daily Costs)

The cost of a taxi ride in Rome is significantly more than public transportation. On average, past travelers have spent €17 per person, per day, on local transportation in Rome.

Food Budget in Rome (Average Daily Costs)

While meal prices in Rome vary, the average daily cost of eating in Rome is €37. Based on past tourists' spending habits, an average lunch in Rome should cost roughly €15 per person while dining out. Breakfast is typically less expensive than lunch or supper. Food costs at Rome's sit-down restaurants are frequently higher than fast food or street food pricing.

Entertainment Budget in Rome (Average Daily Costs)

In Rome, entertainment and activities generally cost €30 per person, per day. This covers entry prices to museums and sites, day trips, and other sightseeing cos Entertainment and activities in Rome typically cost an average of €29 per person, per day. This includes fees paid for admission tickets to museums and attractions, day tours, and other sightseeing expenses.

Tips and Handouts Budget in Rome (Average Daily Costs)

In Rome, the average price for Tips and Handouts is €24 per day. In Rome, the typical tip is between 5% and 15%.

Scams, Robberies, and Mishaps Budget in Rome (Average Daily Costs)

Unfortunately, horrible things may happen when traveling. You'll simply have to deal with it! In Rome, the average cost of a fraud, heist, or mishap is €5.50.

Alcohol Budget in Rome (Average Daily Costs)

In Rome, the typical person spends roughly €15 per day on alcoholic beverages. Despite your bigger budget, the more you spend on booze, the more fun you may have.

Water Budget in Rome (Average Daily Costs)

In Rome, consumers spend €2.71 per day on bottled water. The water at Rome's public fountains is considered safe to drink.

References

Budget Your Trip. (n.d.). *Rome travel cost - average price of a vacation to Rome*. https://www.budgetyourtrip.com/italy/rome

Family Destinations Guide. (n.d.). *17 best hotels in Rome for families*. https://familydestinationsguide.com/best-hotels-rome-families/

In Your Pocket. (n.d.). *Best Western Hotel Universo*. https://www.inyourpocket.com/rome/best-western-hotel-universo_164387v

Living a Life in Colour. (n.d.). *Italian etiquette – when in Rome do as the Romans do*. https://www.livingalifeincolour.com/about/resources/italian-etiquette-when-in-rome-do-as-the-romans-do/

Lonely Planet. (n.d.). *Best time to visit Rome*. https://www.lonelyplanet.com/articles/best-time-to-visit-rome

Milwaukee Public Museum. (n.d.). *Roman Empire: A brief history*. https://www.mpm.edu/research-collections/anthropology/anthropology-collections-research/mediterranean-oil-lamps/roman-empire-brief-history

My Lifelong Holiday. (n.d.). *Secret Rome: 20 hidden gems in Rome you really need to discover*. https://www.mylifelongholiday.com/secret-rome/

My Vacation Itineraries. (n.d.). *4 days in Rome itinerary*. https://myvacationitineraries.com/4-days-in-rome-itinerary/

Pexels. (2017). *Photography of lighted bridge* [Photograph]. https://www.pexels.com/photo/photography-of-lighted-bridge-753639/

PlanetWare. (n.d.). *Top things to do in Rome with kids*. https://www.planetware.com/italy/rome-with-kids-top-things-to-do-i-1-30.htm

Pocket Wanderings. (2023, August 18). *15 best luxury hotels in Rome*. https://www.pocketwanderings.com/best-luxury-hotels-in-rome/

Rolandia. (n.d.). *Useful Romanian phrases for your perfect holiday*. https://rolandia.eu/en/blog/travel-tips/useful-romanian-phrases-for-your-perfect-holiday

Solo Globetrotter. (2021, June 19). *Facts about Rome*. https://thesologlobetrotter.com/facts-about-rome-facts/

The Italian on Tour. (n.d.). *The most affordable boutique hotels in Rome, Italy*. https://www.theitalianontour.com/the-most-affordable-boutique-hotels-in-rome-italy/

Time Out Rome. (2023, February 7). *The 30 best restaurants in Rome*. https://www.timeout.com/rome/restaurants/best-restaurants-in-rome

Top Rated Online. (n.d.). *Worst-rated restaurants in Rome*. https://www.top-rated.online/countries/Italy/cities/Rome/Restaurants/worst-rated

Voyage Tips. (n.d.). *Things to do in Rome: The 35 best places to visit and highlights*. https://www.voyagetips.com/en/things-to-do-in-rome/#1_The_Colosseum_and_its_murderous_games

Wanderlust Chloe. (2021, March 29). *40 fun facts about Rome*. https://www.wanderlustchloe.com/facts-about-rome/

Rome Actually. (n.d.). *Best budget hotels in Rome for a great stay*. https://www.romeactually.com/budget-hotels-in-rome/

Other Quick Guides

Quick Travel Guide to Paris

The City of Light never needs a long introduction, Paris dazzles from the first step. Stroll the Seine at sunset, lose yourself in the Louvre, sip café au lait at a corner bistro, and watch the Eiffel Tower sparkle after dark. From hidden courtyards to grand boulevards, this quick guide makes it easy to unlock the romance, art, and flavor of Paris in one unforgettable trip.

Quick Travel Guide to London

From Big Ben's chimes to hidden corners only locals know, London is a city that never stops surprising. This quick guide gives you the essentials: history, slang, etiquette, attractions, and insider tips, so you can see the capital like a Londoner, not just a visitor.

www.ingramcontent.com/pod-product-compliance
Lightning Source LLC
Chambersburg PA
CBHW071528120626
46550CB00006B/2387